The Fragrance of a Rose

By

Louis Velez

ISBN: 1-4140-0658-6 (e-book)
ISBN: 1-4140-0659-4 (Paperback)

Library of Congress Control Number: 2003098502

This book is printed on acid free paper.

Printed in the United States of America
Bloomington, IN

1stBooks — rev. 02/09/04

Acknowledgments

Thank you

~ Bruce Weigl for helping me edit this book.

~ Louis Nemecio Velez my twin brother for his invaluable support and love throughout my trials in life, you were always there for me.

~ P.O.M.C. for all your help with gathering petitions and letters of encouragements during the trial.

~ Dr. Robert Eppley for all your counseling during the last three years.

~ Shelly Gerek a special thanks for holding my hand through the worst part of my life and for your continuing friendship.

~ Dr. Mark McKinley for his invaluable help

Table of Contents

In loving memory of my daughter
Virginia Rose Velez
1984- 1999.*

Most of the proceeds from the sale of this book will go toward the establishing of "The Virginia Rose Velez Scholarship Fund" and also a portion will be donated to the Parents of Murdered Children Inc.

Introduction

To lose a child is the cruelest thing that can happen to a parent. It doesn't matter how it happens, either through illness or accident, or in my case murder, it is still a loss that will affect you forever. The pain and grief is overwhelming. The depression that follows took me through so many twists, turns, and places I'd never thought I'd be. It made me feel things I'd never felt before.

I have been faced with death before. My father died several years ago. Although I cried and mourned his passing, I went through the grieving process in a short amount of time. Losing my father wasn't an easy thing to go through, however I knew that he was sickly and old. Somehow, knowing he was ill almost justified his passing. He passed away during the night in his sleep.

I am not trying to diminish the death of a parent. I'm merely trying to draw a comparison based on my own personal experience. I still miss my father. I miss his council and advise, but mostly, I miss his companionship. Still, I was able to come to terms with his passing and carry on with my life.

Over the course of the last few years, I have discussed grief with people who have lost love ones. Some had lost their spouses, others, their siblings. Most of them had lost parents and close friends. All had gone through depression, anger, frustration, denial, and grief. Their grief was not the same. Their grief seemed to be the same as mine. But most importantly, they all seemed to have managed to reach a level of acceptance. This was something I could never do. To lose a parent is difficult and many people have experienced this. Yet, people soon learn to accept this loss as the natural order of life and death.

I have become acquainted with an even greater pain, the pain of losing a child. Within this pain, I could find no acceptance. I couldn't remarry to fill a void, nor could I find any inner peace from knowing it was a natural or an expected death. I lost my daughter on the 23rd of November, 1999. Her name was Virginia, To her family and friends, she was known as, "The Rose".

1
My Children

I remember the first time I saw my daughter. She was an innocent, tiny baby. She was pure at heart and full of life. I loved her immediately. I already had two boys, and now I had been blessed with a girl.

If innocence has a smell, that's how I would describe how this tiny baby smelled. She was a fragile little person I would have to protect.

I loved my boys, but I knew that they would take on the rituals of boyhood: playing catch in the backyard and wrestling around in a rough and tumble way, I knew they would be strong. Not so with this little girl. She brought out of me a tenderness I never knew I had. Suddenly, I was more than a father. I had to assume the role of protector.

In just a few short years, that tiny infant had grown into a beautiful, young child. Her hair had thickened and began to form in shiny, healthy waves. She had gained weight. It showed in her pudgy cheeks and nose. Her lips were definitely mine: heart-shaped and full. She would often comment on how our lips looked alike. I saw much of me in her and that made me feel good.

If I had to choose my favorite feature of hers, it would have to be her eyes. Those big, brown, beautiful eyes said everything. When she smiled, her eyes became shiny and bright in a contagious smile that seemed to come from deep in her soul. But look out when she became angry. Those eyes would take on a half-closed look that put you in your place, almost immediately. Mostly, she knew how to use those eyes on me. One look at me with a hint of sadness and I would give in to almost anything she wanted.

She remained tiny. One day, when she was about three years old, she called for me to come pick her up from her mother's house just to spend some time together. I pulled up in the driveway in my shiny, white Eldorado and she was waiting for me. She was dressed in a little blue jean skirt outfit, her favorite clothes. She looked so tiny that, from that day, I called her my "Little Munchkin". I opened the car door and she jumped onto the armrest, her favorite spot that allowed her to see out the window. "Let's roll, pops!" She'd say, and off we'd go. Quickly and surely, we had become very close.

I would hold her close to me, as though I didn't want to let go. Little did I know how one day my heart would break into a million pieces over her; or the countless number of tears I would shed knowing how brutally she would be taken from us.

I have beautiful memories of my daughter. My favorite is when she was about seven years old. By this time, she had gained a considerable amount of weight. Her face had become round and full, yet, it didn't take away from her big, bright eyes or her beautiful smile. She had become a little butterball. Whenever I would be lying on the sofa, she would grab her favorite blanket and lay on top of me. She would whisper in my ear, "I love you daddy", and soon fall fast asleep. My son took a picture of us on the sofa in that position. I treasure that picture because it tells me she was daddy's little girl. Years after, that particular picture would make headline news.

Today, November 21st, 1999, Virginia is turning 15 years old. She had blossomed into a beautiful, young lady. She had shed her baby fat and developed a curvy, young figure. To my disapproval, she began to wear makeup as well. Her hair had grown long and cascaded in a gentle wave off her shoulder.

Somehow, she had grown up, yet, she managed to stay close to me. Every time she'd come to see me, she displayed that beautiful smile that lit up a room. She always remained affectionate towards me, always sitting beside me. 'If I didn't put my arm around her fast enough she would take my arms and put them around her. I liked to tease her about everything just to make her laugh. I would make comments about certain boys I knew she liked. She would attempt to get angry, but she couldn't help but laugh. She had this laugh that made you laugh with her. She'd toss back her head and blast out a big "Ha-Ha-Ha!" You could feel the energy in her happiness.

Sometimes, as I looked at her, I couldn't get over how pretty she' d become. At five feet and one inch, she wasn't very tall, but her unselfish demeanor and her loving ways made her appear larger than life. It more than made up for any lack of which she might have had.

I can remember only a handful of times when I was the target of my daughter's anger. Mostly, it was over her makeup. I didn't approve of all that makeup. The arguments, of course, were short-lived and soon she'd be sitting beside me as though nothing had happened. I would stroke her long, brown hair, kiss her on the cheek and the anger would disappear.

I was eagerly waiting for her today. I had prepared her favorite meal of rice and beans and I had a birthday card with money in it waiting for her. I always gave her money so she could go to the mall and shop with her friends. Shopping at the mall was one of her favorite pastimes.

As I looked out of the front room window, she was there. She was bouncing up the driveway as I had seen her do a hundred times before.

Her mother and I had divorced years ago, but somehow I managed to buy a house right around the corner from where she lived. It was a plan that worked out well. My children were able to come to my house often. I was bound and determined to be a part of their lives, no matter what, even if it meant living around the comer from my ex-wife. Our children had two homes to call theirs, and I would be there for them.

I could see the excitement in Virginia's eyes when she walked into the house. I wished her happy birthday and she said, "Thank you, daddy!" Where's my present?" I handed her the birthday card and laughed as she opened it and quickly pocketed the money. We spent the next couple of hours joking and laughing at pictures of her previous birthdays.

My favorite picture was that of her first birthday. She had on a frilly red dress. She was sitting in her high chair. Her eyes were wide opened as she looked at her birthday cake with one candle on top. The cake appeared to be bigger than her.

We laughed at the picture of her fifth birthday. She wore a party hat in the shape of a cone. I told her it looked like dunce cap. She quickly placed her hand over the picture not wanting us to see it.

When we finished our trip down memory lane, she took some money out of her pocket and began to count it. I quickly stole the money from her hand and ran to my bedroom. She gave chase and began to poke at my sides. "Give me back my money you old fart!" She said. I plopped down onto my bed and hid the money under me. She climbed on top of me and continued tickling and poking my sides until I finally gave in. I handed her the money. I laughed while she counted the money to make sure I wasn't hiding some of it. We sat on the edge of the bed and continued laughing.

"You are going to help me buy a car next year, aren't you daddy?" I said, "Sure Muchkin, and two pillows!" She looked puzzled when I mentioned two pillows. "Why two pillows? She asked. I told her she would need the two pillows to place under her butt so she could see out the window. "Very funny!" She said, as she elbowed me in the ribs.

Later, we sat on the sofa to watch some television. As usual, she took my arm and placed it around her shoulder. A warm feeling came over me. After fifteen years, she still remained daddy's little girl.

She devoured the meal I had prepared for her. She kept going back for more. "Keep eating like that and you're going to look like a blimp!" I said to her. She was obsessed with this new trim figure of hers, and became angry if anyone called her fat. She hated being heavy when she was younger.

I caught the whole day on my new video camera that Kim and the kids bought for my birthday just the week before. Surely, next year we would watch this video on television and laugh at all our antics on her 15th birthday. I kept telling Kim that it was for times like these why I had always wanted a video camera. I wanted to capture the memories so they would always stay clear in my mind. I'm glad I got that camera that year.

While the girls went outside to begin preparations to hang the Christmas lights, I cleaned up around the kitchen. When I finished, I soon joined them. We were going to put the lights and 13 decorations up for the holidays. It had become a tradition, although my sons thought they had become too old for this activity.

Aaron, my oldest son, was 20 years old already. He had grown tall and handsome. I was proud to see him make a life of his own. He had been a jock all through high school, a regular football fanatic. I was sure he was watching today's game with his friends somewhere. He would be over later to discuss the games, as usual.

My son Christopher, the middle child of my first marriage, was quite the opposite of my son Aaron. Actually, Christopher was different from all my children. He was forever in trouble in school. He was always getting suspended for one thing or another. He finally quit school and got a job. I hoped, encouraged, and practically begged him to join the military service or a trade school. I hated seeing him just wasting his life. I was heartbroken over his decisions. What kind of future would he have? At 18, Christopher was old enough to decide things for himself. I was helpless in doing anything about that. I could only hope that one day he would come to realize his mistakes and change the direction of his life.

Today, my fiance Kim, her two children, Virginia and I would hang the Christmas lights ourselves. It was a brisk cold windy day and the sun was shining. We brought out a rickety old ladder and a box of tangled lights. I couldn't help but laugh at everyone trying to untangle that mess of wires and bulbs. They were having a blast. Kim was afraid of heights and Virginia knew this. She kept swaying that old ladder underneath Kim's feet to the point where she had her screaming. I laughed. The other two danced around the yard making a bigger mess. I stood back and videotaped the whole episode. Kim was mad. Finally she said, "Hey, if you're going to stand there and laugh, then go watch the game or something!" It was cold outside anyway, so that's exactly what I did.

Inside the house, I lied on the sofa and began to watch the game. I became tired and fell fast asleep.

I awoke a couple of hours later to find that all the Christmas lights had been hung. Virginia had left to go to a friend's house down the street to collect another birthday present. She had promised to come back for the lighting of the lights they had so proudly hung that would signal the onset of the Christmas season.

When it became dark, everyone assembled in front of the house with the video camera rolling, everyone but Virginia. The entire house was shining with different colored lights. Everyone was ooohing and aahing. I kept thinking how Virginia was missing all the excitement. I wasn't too concerned, though. I was sure she must have gotten caught up in the moment with her friends.

Soon, everyone had gone inside to end the evening and I was left looking up and down the street for Virginia. Even though we had spent a special day together, she had managed to slip away without saying good-bye. That bothered me. I was disappointed, but not overly concerned. I thought that in the excitement of her birthday, she had lost track of time. I was still disappointed.

That night I went to bed knowing that Virginia had been with me most of the day and that we had a great time celebrating her 15th birthday. We all had a good dinner and a wonderful time practicing our Christmas tradition. I looked forward to the following week. I would only have to work three more days. Then, I would be off the Thanksgiving holiday. Kim had already bought the turkey and all the trimmings. It would only be a matter of days before all my children would gather for Thanksgiving dinner. The house will be filled with their laughter and the mouth-watering aroma of all the food cooking would tease us until dinner time.

Monday and Tuesday passed and I still had no word from Virginia. I didn't worry much because I knew she was at her mother's house, which was right around the block. I just assumed she was out spending her birthday money and making plans for the five-day weekend she had coming. I knew I would see her then, so I brushed any concern out of my mind.

For some odd reason Tuesday was a grueling day at work. Part of it was the work itself, it was because of this strange sense of anxiety I felt. It was like no other feeling I had ever experienced before, almost like when I was expecting something to happen. I couldn't wait for the night to end.

Finally, the workday (or night in my case) ended and I made my way home. As I stumbled through the door I headed straight for bed. Normally, I sit up and watch a little TV. And have a snack, but tonight I was completely exhausted and all I wanted to do was enjoy a restful night's sleep. I hadn't the slightest inkling this particular night would be the last time I would have a peaceful rest.

Louis Velez

Virginia's 1st Birthday

2

The Day It All Began

It was Wednesday, November 24th, 1999. I hadn't been asleep for very long when the phone rang. It just kept ringing in the distance. I finally got up and answered it. I expected it to be telemarketers so I growled hello into the phone. It was my ex-wife. Sometimes, I thought I had made a mistake by living around the corner from her. She would call me about every little complaint she had about the children and expect me to come rushing over. Some of her calls were valid, but most were ridiculous nonsense.

This call, however, was different. I sensed urgency, a fear about her voice. I could almost feel her trembling through the phone. She was crying so I asked her what was wrong. She began to tell me that our daughter, Virginia, had not been home all night. I guess she had planned an overnight stay with some girlfriends across the street.

When my ex-wife went there for her this morning, she was told that Virginia had left the night before. She went on to tell me that a girl's body had been found in the woods near where we lived, and that she was certain it was Virginia. She never said why she was so certain and I never asked. She was always certain about everything, even when she was not. I believed it to be another one of her dramatic episodes so I didn't give her words much thought. She had already alerted the police and they were on their way.

"Please come over!" I need you here!" She cried. I said, "I'll be over there in a minute." I still didn't know what to think. I was half asleep, and my ex-wife was known for her being dramatic. Usually, she would call right back to have me disregard her previous call, so I laid there for a minute waiting.

I hung up the phone and got up from the bed, but then sat right back down. I felt a feeling in my knees. My knees felt weak and shaky, almost too weak to stand on. Finally, I got up and made my way to the kitchen. I figured, I would make a cup of coffee, and by the time I was finished she would surely call back to tell me that everything had been a false alarm, just one big mistake, and that our daughter was safe in school.

The phone rang again just as I expected. This time, to my surprise, it was my son, Aaron.

"Dad!" He cried. "Please come over … we need you!" I quickly dressed and rushed out of the house. I was there in minutes. I opened the door and walked in to find my ex-wife sitting on the couch, trembling and crying. She kept saying "I know it's her! I know it's her, my baby!"

There were two detectives there. One looked as if he had just graduated from high school. He looked too young to be a detective. He had a baby face. He wore a baseball cap with no sign of facial hair. He didn't wear any worry, like you would see in a more seasoned detective. He was tall and slim. He was dressed in jeans, a jacket, and gym shoes. The brim of his cap hid any expression on his face.

The other man was burly looking with a thick, brown mustache. He wore his hair straight back with a perfect part down the middle. I seemed to focus on his words, maybe it was because he was closer to my age and I felt I could relate to him more. This detective was holding some photographs in his hands that were taken at the crime scene, so far, their only evidence.

He handed me the pictures and warned me by saying, "They're very graphic Sir." Hesitating, I took the pictures from his hand. I looked at the first photograph. It was of a young girl lying lifeless on the ground. She had been stripped of all her clothes. She lay there in her underclothes with one shoe on. I quickly handed the pictures back to the detective.

"I can't be certain," I said. "I just can't be certain."

My son and ex-wife refused to view the photos. It was up to me. As I was handing back the stack of pictures, they both stared at me, as if asking if it was Virginia. I just shook my head and said, "No, I can't be certain."

The burly detective asked me if I would be willing to go to the morgue to make a positive identification. I didn't want to go, but someone had to. I had to know for sure. The police had to know for sure too. I agreed to go to the morgue. I asked my son to accompany me. I knew it couldn't be my Virginia, so I went. The detectives said they would meet us there. Meanwhile, a victim's advocate was on her way to my ex-wife's house and would arrive soon to accompany us.

While I waited for the advocate to arrive, I stood there and looked out of the front room window. I prayed to see Virginia come home before the advocate arrived. My son was standing beside me, and every now and then he'd put his arm around me, to comfort me for what lay ahead. A neighbor had come over. She sat on the sofa beside my ex-wife to try and comfort her as she sat there crying and trembling with fear.

My mind was a total blank. All I could do was look out the window. I tried to look up and down the street. I kept saying to myself, "Virginia, please come home," After standing there for what seemed like an eternity, a strange car pulled into the driveway. I was hoping it was someone dropping off my little girl. I began to think that she and a car full of friends had decided to skip school and she was now coming home to face her punishment. I hoped it was a secret love, someone she was too afraid to tell us about so she went off with him, not telling in fear of being kept away from him. I had a feeling of relief and anger about me. I held my breath as I waited for her to exit the car. When she walked threw the door, I was going to hold her tight then really let her have it for all the worry she had caused. To my disappointment, it was the advocate we had been waiting for. She approached the door, announced who she was, and I invited her in. She was a slender, short woman with blonde hair. As she walked in, I looked out the door to see if anyone, hopefully Virginia, might be following her. I didn't know it then, but she would be at my side throughout the course of events that would follow.

I rode with her while my son followed us in my truck. The morgue was in the basement of one of the local hospitals. The ride there was a long, silent one. It suddenly dawned on me what I was doing. I didn't know where I was going. I didn't know what I was doing riding with a lady I didn't even know. I wanted to jump out of her car and go home. I had just been with Virginia on Sunday. She had been fine and very happy. Surely, it couldn't be her. If something had been wrong, she would have told me. It was too late, though.

We arrived at the hospital and parked. My son, Aaron, parked nearby, and I summoned him over to help me walk. That strange feeling in my knees had returned, even stronger than before. I don't know if I needed his help to walk or just the presence of his strength beside me. He put his arm in mine and we walked to the hospital entrance.

The same detectives that were at my ex-wife's house were standing in the hospital lobby, waiting to meet with us. Another gentleman was with them. I learned later he was the coroner. We were led down a long hallway and down two flights of stairs. We came to a huge, gray door where everyone stopped.

"This is the morgue, "I thought. As the coroner began to unlock the door, he looked at me and warned me not to touch anything. Immediately, my son and the advocate took a tight hold of my arms.

The door was slightly opened when I caught a glimpse of that beautiful, brown hair I used to love to stroke. I didn't need to look any further, but they managed to take me closer where I saw my daughter's face. Even though it had been partially covered, I could see it was Virginia. Her big, brown eyes that had once lit up a room were now tightly closed. I saw her lips that looked like mine. She was my Virginia. I felt a pain in my heart as it broke into a million little pieces while I looked at her. I wasn't allowed to touch her. I wasn't even allowed to kiss her good-bye. I nodded my head at the detectives to confirm the identity of my child. Immediately, I was pulled out of the room and back into the hallway. The gray door slammed shut behind me. I knew then that my life would never be the same. Joy and gladness had escaped my being and sorrow took their place.

My son and I walked back down the long hallway. Neither one of us said a word. My head swam with thoughts of everything, yet nothing at all.

"What do I do, now?" I thought. "Where do I go?"

As we drove home, I looked over at my son every now and then. I knew he was ready to blow. He had to drive us home. The sensation that had been in my knees had now spread through my entire body. I couldn't drive. When we finally pulled into his mother's driveway, my son gave in. He began to cry and scream and pound the steering wheel.

"No! No!" He kept yelling. He stumbled out of the truck, jumped into his car and sped off, leaving me alone to break the news to his mother.

I opened the door. She looked at me and no words were needed. She saw the look on my face that confirmed her worst fears. I walked over to her and we held each other. Her knees buckled and I helped her to a chair. By this time, some friends of hers gathered at the house. I knew that if I left she would be all right.

"I have a lot to do now." I said, and I left to return home. When I got there, I walked straight into the garage. Tears began to roll down my face and onto the garage floor. I cried so hard that I began to gasp for air. I looked around to find that I was alone. The police called Kim's work but she still didn't come. I kept wondering when she was going to get home. I wanted her to go to the morgue with me. I needed her to be here for me now. I later learned that her employer decided to give her the urgent message four hours later. Any messages received during business hours were given to the employees on their personal time. So they waited for Kim's lunch hour to give her the message. The Chief of Police made the call to the company and he explained the nature of the emergency. Kim, was only told to call home on her lunch hour. I was all alone with an emptiness that would never again be filled.

I felt for some reason, I was being punished. All of my pass sins and transgressions had finally caught up with me, and I was facing the consequences of those misdeeds. For the rest of my life, I would suffer with the guilt that had suddenly overcome me. But I wondered who was punishing me. Was it God? Impossible, I thought. My God is not a cruel God. He is a God of love, compassion, and mercy. I knew I had to let go of that feeling because my God would never do such a terrible thing to me, ever! I knew it was not the will of God, but the actions of a sick, sadistic monster.

I had to call someone to be with me. Surely, I would lose my mind. I found the strength to go into the house and call my twin brother who lived down the street. I knew he would come right away, and he did. He walked into the garage where I had returned. He knew I was crying. He asked what was wrong.

"They've killed my little girl … Virginia!" I said.

His face twisted into a look of agony. He threw his hat onto the garage floor and began to cry. We cried and held each other. I heard him begin to pray and I joined him:

"Lord, allow this child into your kingdom." He said. "Our Father, who art in Heaven, hallowed be thy name, thy kingdom come, thy will be done, on earth as it is in Heaven. Give us this day, our daily bread, and forgive us our debts, as we also forgive our debtors. And lead us not into temptation, but deliver us from evil…"

My brother spoke the words as I went along with them in my mind. He went on to ask the Lord to reach down and comfort us, and for it all to be one big mistake. We said, Amen, and them embraced.

After awhile it seemed as if we had been crying forever, we began to compose ourselves and talk. We decided that the rest of the family had to be told, especially our mother. She was elderly and we weren't sure how she'd handle the loss of her granddaughter. My brother entered my house and began calling family members. I couldn't bear to utter the words again, so he spoke for me. My oldest brother was the first to be called. He was the one who had personally gone to tell my mother. Just as I expected, she broke down and began to have chest pains. Thankfully, it wasn't a heart attack. She demanded to be taken to me, so my brother brought my mother to my house. She was frail and weak, but she managed to deal with the heartbreak.

Soon, my family had all began to gather at my home. By this time, Kim had come home. She was in shock to say the least. I believe it was the shock that kept her from breaking down. She shed a few tears and held her head up strong. I'm glad she did. I couldn't bear to see her torn apart. I needed her strength. My brothers were the first to arrive. Then Kim's mother came over to comfort us. Periodically, neighbors would stop in for a brief condolence. Next, all my nieces and nephews came by. I hadn't seen them in ages. They'd come in and break down the minute they entered the house. Last to arrive was my daughter Leigh. Her mother had brought her over because she wanted to be with me during this tragic time.

My head began to ache from all the noise of voices echoing with laughter, crying and chatting. Kim made sure that everyone was comfortable. She answered their questions so I would not have to talk about what had happened. She took care of everything. I was very appreciative that she could take control over this situation. I was in no condition to console anyone because I was consumed with grief of my own. Kim stayed busy tending to all of our family and friends.

Even though she was stricken by these tragic events, she managed to stay strong. I knew she was doing it for me. I also knew that when our guest would leave, she would break down, too. Virginia called her "mom" and Kim loved her dearly. Over the years, they had become very close.

At 5 o'clock, the news came on. The media finally had a name and a face to place with the story they were running about my daughter since that morning. As the newsman told the story of a young girl that had been found dead and burned in the woods of a local neighborhood, a picture of my daughter was flashed on the screen and her name was spoken. My ex-wife had given the police a recent picture of my daughter. The media got their hands on it immediately. I couldn't bear to watch. I buried my face in my son's chest and cried uncontrollably. The news failed to mention if anyone had been arrested. As of yet, there were no suspects.

"What kind of monster would do such a thing?" I thought. "What demon would brutally take my daughter from me?" Whoever did this would answer to me.

It was getting late and the house began to slowly empty out. My sons left with the promise to return the next day. My nine year old, Tyler and my stepdaughter, Elena had gone to bed. My daughter, Leigh, and her mother were about to leave too. I hugged Leigh tightly and begged her to be careful. I kissed her goodnight and soon she was gone. Everyone else had left about the same time.

Kim and I were finally alone. We sat beside each other in the darkness, neither one of us knowing what to say. We were tired and very sleepy, but we just kept sitting there holding each other in silence.

All I could think was why? Why would anyone want to hurt my little girl? Better yet, who? Who was this monster? There were so many questions but no answers. As it would turn out, some of these questions would never be answered. We finally made it to bed that night. I tossed and turned just thinking about the events of the day.

"Please, God!" I prayed. "God, let me find that today had just been one cruel nightmare, that my daughter would be at home safe and sound." "Please, God!"

I couldn't take it anymore. I got out of bed. I drank coffee and smoked one cigarette after another. I sat there waiting for an appropriate time to call my ex-wife. I couldn't wait any longer. I picked up the phone and dialed. I told her that I was calling, just in case all of this had been a big mistake and that maybe, Virginia had come home.

"No" she said. I hung up the phone and began to look out of the front room window. I yelled her name, hoping she would hear me and come home. Reality had started to take hold and I began to lose control of myself. I sat down on the sofa with tears streaming down my face.

"It's true." I said to myself. "My little girl is gone." It was Thanksgiving Day, but all that had been bought for the celebration we had planned just sat in the kitchen uncooked and unprepared. This year, there would be no Thanksgiving celebration.

3

The Funeral

We were made to wait a couple of days. The coroner had to make a finding as to the actual cause of death before he would let me have Virginia.

It was Friday, mid-morning, when I looked out the window to see policemen everywhere. I went to the kitchen to open the door and one by one they marched into my house. Most of them were people I knew from high school, and they had come to offer their condolences. The Chief of Police came in last and hugged me. We'd grown up together and still remained good friends, but I knew this visit wasn't a social one. He had news I'd been waiting to hear. Without making any eye contact with me, he told me the name of the man they had arrested in connection with my daughter's murder. The police accumulated enough evidence to charge him with aggravated murder, gross abuse of a corpse, and tampering with evidence. He was in custody and being held on an extremely high bond.

There was, yet, another twist to his story. Apparently, a juvenile had also been arrested in the case. However, due to the stupidity of the juvenile court judge, he had been released to the custody of his father. He was still under investigation, but a quick arrest was needed so the police had arrested him on tampering with evidence charges. The judge read only the charges, without reviewing the case file, and failed to realize that his arrest was in connection with a murder so she set him free. I was furious. The chief saw the look on my face and quickly assured me he'd do everything he could to get this kid locked up again. On that note, they all began to leave. The Chief, once again, hugged me and offered his condolences before he walked out the door.

That day, the police left me with two names I had never heard before. I thought I knew all of Virginia's friends, but I never heard her mention these two names. I wondered who they were. Most importantly, I wondered how it was possible that she could have become acquainted with these two monsters, or how she had found her way to the murderer's house. I learned that the murder had taken place in the basement of the duplex where the killer lived. The juvenile went by the nickname, T.C. I never learned what those initials stood for. I learned the name of the monster that had taken my daughter from me, but I refuse to utter it from my lips or print it in the pages of this book. By doing so, I would be acknowledging this monster a human. I would be accepting him as a person. This was no person and there was nothing humane about what he had done. To me he is is a sick, twisted, sadistic demon. I will refer to him as the demon monster.

I had so many questions in my head that day. What had transpired? Had she been lured there somehow? How did she end up in the basement? Most importantly, why? Although I learned the answers to some of these questions, the answers still made no sense. Unfortunately, some of these questions remain unanswered.

It was almost 5 o'clock when the coroner called. Kim answered the phone, but he wanted to speak to me.

"We determined the cause of death." He said. "I wanted to tell you first before the media became aware of it."

I found out that my daughter had died as a result of strangulation. I didn't mean to be rude, but after hearing the coroner say the word strangulation, I hung up the phone abruptly. I stood their frozen. A feeling of helplessness and failure came over me. I failed to be there to protect her, and now, I was helpless in doing anything about it. The law had tied my hands. Vengeance was out of the question.

In silent anger, I made my way to the bedroom. I fell on my knees, but not in prayer. I agonized over the thought of how my little girl must have suffered in her last moments. I wished I'd never been told how she died. Now, I would have to deal with another aspect of my daughter's death. There, in the silence of my bedroom, I began to cry once more but in an angry way. It was an anger I had never known before.

I can't remember how long I had been in my bedroom. I had lost track of time. Kim came in and knelt down beside me. Now that the cause of death had officially been established, her body could be released and a funeral home had to be chosen. Kim said not to worry, that she had already taken care of the matter. She had made an early morning appointment with the funeral director. I began to dread the thought of going. I knew that tomorrow I would have to face even more reality.

That night I couldn't sleep and I tossed and turned again and again. Finally in frustration, I got up and went into the living room. Everyone had fallen asleep and I sat there in quiet loneliness, waiting for the morning. At some point, I must have dozed off. Kim woke me up with a cup of coffee in her hand.

"Drink your coffee and get in the shower," she said, "we have to leave soon." When we arrived at the funeral home, my ex-wife and her husband were already there. The funeral director led us into his office. He seemed to be a kind man. He was a short, rather stout gentleman. He looked familiar. I knew I had seen him before. Suddenly, it came to me that this was the same funeral home where, years ago, my father's funeral services had been held.

He had the four of us take a seat around his desk. Immediately, he began to ask questions about Virginia: her hobbies, daily rituals, interests, and school. He asked about brothers, sisters, and other family members. I didn't know it then, but he was preparing her obituary. He showed us a catalog containing sympathy cards and other things we might be interested in buying in Virginia's honor. I was only half-paying attention. I still refused to believe I was there planning a funeral for one of my beloved children. I sat back in silence and allowed Virginia's mother to choose whatever she liked.

The funeral director asked us to follow him. He led us to a flight of stairs. He proceeded to climb the stairway and directed us to come with him. At the top of the stairs was a huge room filled with caskets. I froze in the entrance, not wanting to take another step. I could see my ex-wife looking at one. It had roses on the handles and a tint of copper in the shiny white finish.

She turned to me and asked, "How's this one?"

I didn't say a word. I walked slowly over to the white casket and placed my hand on it. Tears began to pour from my eyes and fall onto the casket as I thought about my precious child and how she would rest there forever. I left the building, not wanting to continue the business that was left. There was not much left to say or do and I knew Kim would handle the rest of it on my behalf.

A short while later, Kim emerged from the building. She told me that the services would be held the next day from two to four o'clock and again from seven until 9 o'clock that evening. The funeral would be the following day. We had already made arrangements at the cemetery where she would be entombed in a mausoleum.

There was another stop we had to make, the flower shop. There was only one choice to make … the roses. A few months before my daughter was murdered, she had made a comment about how she wanted her funeral to look. It was just in conversation, mainly because I kept teasing her about how one day I'd be gone and she'd feel bad for calling me an old man and making fun of my gray hair.

Out of the blue, she began to speak about how when she passed, she wanted to have beautiful roses surrounding her. Virginia took pride in her middle name, "Rose". She had a love for roses. They were her symbol. The rose is as beautiful as she, and seeing roses made her feel that beauty within. We had to get her the roses she wanted. It was her middle name and the flower that most resembled her likeness. I wanted her likeness to be everywhere so people would remember what a beautiful and loving person she was. Then we picked several different arrangements to fill the room. She would have roses everywhere.

Looking back, I wonder why that particular conversation took place. Normally, when speaking about death, Virginia would get scared and angry over the mere mention of death. She wanted to believe that everyone she loved would somehow live forever. She couldn't bear to think she would have to experience death herself. If anyone ever talked about it, she would cry and beg for the conversation to stop. That day, however, she spoke about it calmly and using many details. I'm glad she told me what she wanted. Beyond my pain I felt a sense of pride in giving her all the roses she wanted.

No parent should ever have to face arranging a child's funeral. It is too cruel. I kept thinking, we should be planning birthday parties, proms, graduations and wedding celebrations, events that fill your life with joy and gladness, instead of, sorrow and grief.

I knew I still had two more days to battle. A battle I knew I couldn't win. I knelt down by my bed and prayed for God too give me the strength for what I was about to endure. I prayed for all of us who have lost a child.

"Give us comfort, Lord." Gather us in your arms … embrace us with your love," I cried.

The day was done. Darkness had fallen and I tried to go to sleep. I knew that tomorrow would be very straining and I needed every bit of energy to get through these days. As exhausted as I had become, I just couldn't get comfortable. Tossing and turning had become a ritual and soon I found myself in the living room and on the sofa again. In the silence of that room, I turned to prayer again. I looked toward the end table and picked up the Bible that was just laying there. It opened to the Twenty-third Psalm. I began reading and it gave me some comfort. I will always believe that God turned to that page for me, always. I sat there and read the Twenty-third Psalm over and over until I fell asleep.

Morning came and, as usual, Kim was there with my coffee. I thought about what lay ahead that day, but at the same time I felt a little comfort in knowing that God himself, had spoken to me through the Twenty-third Psalm. I knew he'd be there holding my hand.

It was almost time to go to the funeral home. Kim and I drove in silence. I think I was afraid not knowing how I'd react and I knew she was too.

When we arrived, there were a few people from the media lurking around the corners. Kim and I hurried for the doors in the rear of the funeral home to avoid any confrontation. The rest of the family was standing in the lobby, waiting for us to arrive. Now that we were here, the service could begin. We alerted the funeral director of our presence, and at that point, he opened the doors to where my daughter laid and led us in. Kim held me by one arm, my brother held the other. I walked slowly to where the casket was, hoping that by the time I got there, I'd wake up from this horrible nightmare.

The wake and the funeral had to be closed casket. I never saw for myself, but we were told that the bums my daughter sustained were so severe, an open casket service was not possible. I was glad the casket was closed. I am sure I would not have made it ifI had to see one of my children lying there.

I got closer to the big, white casket. It was covered in the big spray of roses I had chosen. In the center, directly on top, were some pictures of Virginia placed gently in the bed of roses. At each end were more beautiful arrangements in all sorts of colors. In every direction were pictures and gifts that were brought by people to show their love. Pictures, poems, letter, collages, drawings, and little tokens. Each one displayed a special sentiment, each one demonstrating my daughter's beautiful and loving qualities.

I placed my hand on the spot where her face would be I bent over and kissed it, but I couldn't get up. I laid my head on the casket and cried. I felt my brother's hand stroking my head and Kim's hand rubbing my back. I just laid my head there until Kim led me to take a seat. It wasn't until then that I truly realized how many flowers were there. Roses were everywhere, just as she had wanted. Off to the side, I noticed that my ex-wife had a six-foot display in my daughter's memory. It was filled with pictures from infancy to the day of her fifteenth birthday. It showed every step in her life that she took and she had grown over the years.

People began to file in, mostly relatives, friends, neighbors and acquaintances. Every once in awhile, I'd get up and go up to the casket and kiss it. I would stand there not believing that my daughter was inside. My ex-wife would tell me to sit down, but I didn't want to. Kim insisted that I do whatever I felt most comfortable doing, so I stayed there next to Virginia. Kim would greet the guests and move them around me to keep everyone moving in an orderly fashion passing the casket. So that my ex-wife wouldn't complain about me standing near my daughter.

Two hours passed quickly. Kim came over to me and said, "Honey, let's go home and rest, we have to come back at seven." I don't remember driving there, but Kim and I made it home. When we got home I had this strange feeling that I had left my daughter unattended and unprotected. I was anxious to return, to stand guard over her and let her know that her dad was there. It was already past five o'clock and I felt like it had been hours since I'd left. By six o'clock, I couldn't take it anymore so I returned to the funeral home. The funeral director was very understanding, so he let me in.

I went right to the casket. There, again, I kissed and touched it. This time, since I had some privacy, I talked to her.

"How am I ever going to make it without you Munchkin?" How am I going to live knowing you won't be with me?" I whispered. Silently, I began to really ask myself just how would my life continue without her?

Kim came over. She said there were a lot of people here and they wanted to pay their respects. She led me to a seat. Just then I saw my daughter, Leigh pass a group of people, so I rushed over to where she was seated. I felt a little comfort knowing she was there and I held her hand tightly.

I did nothing but sit there and stare at her. I had lost sight of Kim. When I finally raised my head to look for her, I noticed that a large crowd had gathered that evening. Most of them were Virginia's friends from school. They were all hugging each other and crying. The crowd had spilled into the hallway and into the next room. I was told there was a line of people outside, in the front, back, and down the street. There were policemen everywhere, some in their uniforms and others were in plain clothes.

Most of the people managed to make their way over to me. Some said words of sympathy and gave condolences, while others just shook my hand and said nothing at all. Virginia's high school principal was one of these people. He came over to me, shook my hand, and said, "We're going to miss that little girl." All of her teachers were there too, even teachers from her elementary school years. All of them displayed that utter look of disbelief at what had happened to this sweet little child. Several other people approached me that night. Most of whom I'd never laid eyes on before. It was difficult for me to find any words at all, let alone something that could ease their sadness, so I asked Kim to greet them for me. I wasn't trying to be rude, but each tear I saw made it harder for me to keep it together. Each handshake or pat on the back made my knees want to buckle.

It was already after nine o'clock. More people were still arriving. The funeral director and his staff began politely telling people to leave. Leigh and her mother were leaving too. I hugged her close, not wanting to let her go.

"We'll be here in the morning," her mother said as they both left. With Kim by my side, I walked over and kissed her through the top of the casket. I knew it would be the last time. Tomorrow I would have to begin life without my daughter.

The next morning, the huge crowd that had gathered the evening before was there again. This time, the media was everywhere. In any direction you looked, there was a camera waiting to capture someone's grief for the news. The press was polite, not trying to approach us, but were still taking advantage of every opportunity to publicize this sad private moment. Again, we dashed to the nearest entrance to avoid having our picture taken. So many people were there that all the other parlor rooms were filled with our family and friends. The basement was packed full of people, shoulder to shoulder, hoping to hear over an intercom system. The entire building inside and out, was surrounded with people trying to hear. There were not enough seats for everyone, so most of them had to stand.

Kim and I took a seat in the front row. Leigh sat beside me with her mother next to her. I looked for my sons and found them sitting behind me. I sat there holding on to Leigh as I did the night before. Kim took comfort from a friend of mine who was sitting on the other side of her. While we all sat there waiting for the pastor to begin speaking, someone grabbed my shoulders from behind. It was my dearest and closest friend Roy. He had been here the night before, but couldn't get over to me because of the crowd. He leaned over to me and said, "I'm here for you brother, if you need me." Roy had always been there for me and now, on my darkest day, he was there for me once more.

A pastor from my former church was invited to speak and he opened the service. He read, in a soft, loving tone, some inspirational passages from the Bible. He spoke about the pain he felt for my family as tears rolled down his cheek. He was trying to teach us about grief and reassure us that it was God who was going to bring us through this. He concluded his sermon with a very beautiful prayer that must have made a lot of people open their hearts to God that day.

Silence fell over the crowd as the pastor from my fiance's church made her way to the podium. Kim had asked her to be the person to lead the services. Kim was confident that she would express all the qualities my daughter possessed in a fashion that would give Virginia honor, dignity, respect, and the love she deserved.

The pastor began the service with a prayer. She immediately followed by reciting the obituary that was in all of the newspapers. She made mention of every person that Virginia considered her family.

She shared with the congregation how easy my daughter was to get to know because of her friendliness, cheerfulness, and her upbeat personality. She spoke of the love that Virginia had for everyone and at that moment, I looked around the room and saw all the love everyone had for her.

The sister of the pastor, who has the voice of an angel, took the podium and began to sing a song that told the story about a perfect rose, Jesus Christ. Not knowing the history behind Virginia and the rose, she sang that song like it was meant especially for Virginia. She had three perfect roses in her hand for each verse of the song. As she reached the refrain that ended each verse, she took a rose from her hand and plucked each petal from it. Gently, she crushed the petals in her fingertips and its fragrance filled the air.

At the end of the song the pastor took the podium again. She recited some scriptures, then she began her eulogy with the words, "Virginia was the rose in the vase," as she pointed to a rose-filled vase on the podium before her.

She went on to talk about how my daughter lived and died like the rose. "Roses are a very fragrant flower." She said. "The fragrance that comes from them is lovely." So when you take and crush the petals of a rose, the rose becomes more fragrant and the scent is lovelier than if the rose had been left in tact.

Virginia Rose Velez is that rose whose bud had been plucked in her youth. Her life has been crushed, but her powerful fragrance will live in our hearts and minds. It will live in the memories of Virginia that we carry with us. We will be able to smell the sweet fragrance of Virginia's life and the dear memories will live forever."

She followed this story by telling us of the perfect rose, Jesus Christ. She spoke from John 3:16 and told the story of how Jesus was crushed like a rose and it is because of His sweet fragrance that my Virginia is in Heaven with Him now.

With that comforting message, her sister took the podium again. Upon my request, she began to sing the hymn, "How Great Thou Art." On her first high note, the entire group inside, outside and down below, began to sob uncontrollably. Their voices cried out above hers. It was at that moment the pain kicked in and I lost what little strength I had left. It was the most beautiful song I had ever heard. Each time she said the words, "Then Sings My Soul," I could hear and feel the souls pouring out around me, including my own. When she finished the song, a quiet echo of sobbing and moaning carried on as the pastor returned to the podium to conclude the service. She opened her Bible, read several passages from the book of Psalms, and read a poem called, "Roses Will Bloom Again," and said the final prayer. Her sister took the podium one last time to sing a lullaby that she sang to the infant child she lost.

Without knowing the story behind the song, everyone who was in attendance that day felt her emotion so deeply, they began to grab hold of their children and loved ones as if they too knew the pain of losing a child. It was now time to lay my daughter to rest.

Everyone gathered in front of the funeral home. Television cameras moved in to get a shot of the pallbearers putting the casket into the hearse. The director and his assistants loaded the top of the hearse with all the beautiful roses. We were instructed to go to our vehicles and line up for the procession. Red and blue lights began to flash everywhere, as the local police blocked off all area traffic and lined up to lead the procession. Several local police officers took places with their cars in the front, along side, and in the back of us with their lights flashing.

The line was very long. We kept looking back, Kim and I, to see if everyone was coming. We lost track of the end because people kept joining in. There was no end in sight. It was a very long slow line that kept roads and traffic blocked for a very long time.

The cemetery that my ex-wife chose was far away. We had to go through three towns to get there. As we traveled that long journey. I kept looking at that gold hearse ahead of me. Snow was beginning to fall on the roses that were lying on top of it. As we left our hometown and crossed over into the next, there were more police with their lights flashing, waiting for us to come. As they held back the traffic, each one would join the line as we traveled down the road. The same thing happened in the other town. By the time we arrived, there were cars as far as the eye could see surrounded by blue and red flashing lights and news vans.

We exited our car and stood in the bitter cold as we waited for all the cars to finish entering the cemetery's driveway. Finally we all gathered in front of the chapel where the mausoleum was located. I stood there and watched as the pallbearers took my little girl from the back of the hearse and began carrying her to her final resting place. We all followed behind them in a slow, single-file line. There were few seats available. The immediate family took seats at the benches that were provided while the others crowded in around us. I began to feel like I couldn't breathe.

Another pastor, this time from my ex-wife's church, took a place near the front of the room next to my daughter and began to speak. He went on, preaching to all the young people in the crowd about saving their souls now. By this time, I was very tired and I didn't think I could hold out much longer. I sat there, praying for him to finish so I could end this horrible day. Kim's pastor said a final prayer that gave my daughter her last rights so that she may have peace.

All the people began to line up to say their last good-byes. I waited behind as I watched them cry, pray, and take a rose from the top of the casket. I wanted to be the last to say good-bye. During this time, a gentleman in a gold blazer came up to me and handed me the key to Virginia's casket and walked away with his head down. I continued to stand there while people came up to hug me upon leaving. Finally, it was my turn. I stood there, dreading this moment. I wasn't ready to say good-bye.

A man looked at me and said it was time to place her in the tomb and asked me if I wanted to stay. I knew if I did I would break into a million pieces. Kim and I walked over to my Munchkin to begin our final good-byes. At that moment, I collapsed onto the casket lid, begging her to come back. I cried and pleaded with her to come back to me. I told her repeatedly how much I loved her. Kim took me by my arm and led me away.

I don't remember getting home that day. All I remember is lying in bed that night thinking that tomorrow was the first day I'd have to officially live with my daughter gone. I didn't know how I would make it without her.

4

The Day I Met Satan

Though brokenhearted and still in disbelief, I had managed to make it through the agony of the funeral. I didn't have a clue as to what lay ahead for me in the coming year. I only knew that my life would be empty without my daughter. Life for me would never be the same.

I knew that I would soon be facing even more agony, distress, and even greater anguish. I would have to meet face to face with the monster that killed my daughter. I would have to sit in a trial and listen to the horrible details I didn't want to hear. I wasn't sure if I had enough sanity left in me to hear the story unfold, the story of how my daughter had been brutally murdered. It was bad enough that I had to see my daughter lying in the morgue, lifeless, a picture I can never erase from my mind. The last thing I wanted to see was the gruesome photos the police detectives took at the crime scene blown up into life-size images. Most of all, I didn't want to have the image of that monster's face etched into my thoughts, haunting me forever.

As if this wasn't bad enough, I would have to attend the trial of the juvenile who had witnessed and participated in my daughter's death. He was a big part of this case too. It ate at me daily to think he was free and roaming the streets. I still had a long road ahead of me. I just didn't know how long it was or how many twists and turns it would take. Before all this was to begin, I had to meet with the prosecutor. I was anxious to know about the evidence that had been collected by the police. Up to this point, no one had bothered to tell us anything. I wanted to know how strong our case was.

It was December and the Christmas holidays would soon be upon us. I watched Kim and the kids put up the Christmas tree and begin decorating with different kinds of ornaments. They wrapped presents in colorful foiled wrapping paper and slid them under the tree. Although the tree they had prepared was beautiful, with all the blinking lights and adornments, to me it was empty knowing that this would be the first time there would be no presents under it for Virginia.

The holiday season came and left with little fanfare. The kids enjoyed themselves and they received everything they had hoped for. At the forefront of my thoughts were the days that lay ahead. The day I'd meet the killer was drawing near. I began to mark the days on the calendar just to make sure how long I had. I wasn't going to let this day sneak up on me. I had to be prepared. I didn't know how I'd react to seeing him, and there was no way I could really prepare myself for what I was about to encounter. Still, I had to try anyway.

My first effort of preparation was to meet with the prosecutor who would be trying the case. Kim and I arrived at his office, downtown and we were kept waiting in the tiny room they called the lobby. I remember thinking to myself how drab this little lobby was. Everything from the walls to the floors was the dullest dark brown. Only a few chairs lined the walls. The one thing that really caught my attention was a wall that was covered with pictures of all the former prosecutors dating back to the early 1900's. The furniture consisted of nothing more than a filing cabinet, brown plastic chairs, and an old coffee table lined with outdated magazines to occupy my mind.

I was anxious to meet with this particular criminal prosecutor. He had successfully prosecuted hundreds of cases and was responsible for sending them all to lengthy prison terms. He made no plea bargains. He fought his battles in court. I was confident in his abilities and I felt a sense of loyalty about him. Maybe it had something to do with the fact that he had successfully tried and convicted some of his own colleagues, a police chief, and even a mayor. He had become somewhat of a legend in the legal field. Mostly, he had a penchant for prosecuting corrupt officials. This man only saw black and white, the letter of the law.

Some newspaper articles, however, were not too flattering when it came to reporting his conquests. They called him arrogant, insolent, and downright rude. I never thought I'd have the opportunity to meet him, nor did I really want to, especially under these circumstances. Yet, I was suddenly anxiously waiting to meet him. I was a little unnerved by what the press had to say about him, but I thought if I wanted someone fighting for me, these things would be the attributes I would look for in a prosecutor. I wanted a fighter and he was the one.

After much waiting, his secretary came out and called for us. She led us to his office near a cluster of cubicles. He was bigger than life. He appeared taller than I had imagined. He was going bald and what hair he did have left was turning gray. His brimmed glasses made him look even more professional than the pictures I'd seen in the newspaper.

He rose to greet us and extended his hand toward me. I shook his hand and he asked us to have a seat. He spoke firmly and with authority as he poured over reports from the coroner, the police, and witness accounts about the defendant. He looked toward me and asked if there was anything I knew or would like to add. I got the feeling that he thought all this was familiar to me, somehow. I told him no, that I had never heard about this guy until now. Virginia had never mentioned his name to me.

As our afternoon meeting ended, I stood to shake his hand again and I couldn't help but to notice some kindness and sympathy in those otherwise piercing eyes of his. He too had children and I think he knew how I felt. He said not to worry, that this guy is all but cooked and soon he will be on his way to prison forever. Although he had been called cold and ruthless, at the very moment I couldn't agree. He seemed genuine and concerned. I felt confident he should prevail in this case.

The first hearing for the defendant, that we were allowed to attend, was scheduled for mid-January. Before I knew it, I had less than a week to prepare myself for the confrontation. How? I didn't know. What would go through my mind once I laid eyes on this demon? What would I do? I had already been warned to keep my mouth shut and my hands to myself. I didn't know if I had the strength to control myself.

The morning of the hearing came. I was up early as usual. Anymore, getting up early had become a ritual for me. I kept getting up at all hours of the night and going back to bed. This time when I awoke in the night, I stayed up, waiting for the time we'd have to be in court. My mind was racing with all these thoughts of what I would say or do. I was a nervous wreck. Kim finally got up and began to get ready. I paced around the house, stopping only to check the time.

At my insistence, we left early. I wanted to make absolutely sure that we'd be there. The closer we came to the courthouse the more nervous and fidgety I became. I parked the truck and quickly got out. Kim had to hurry to catch up with me. I was anxious to get into that building and begin the hearing.

As I began to climb the stairs to the entrance, I looked at the courthouse, a huge old sandstone building. We didn't know exactly how to get there, so a victim's advocate from the county offices showed us the way. She led us down a dimly lit stairway to a very narrow hallway. She pointed to a door and informed us that this is where the hearing was to be held. The hallway near the hearing room were lined with plastic chairs. There was barely enough room to walk, let alone pace. The hallway soon began to fill with people who were waiting for other court cases to begin. My family began to gather, along with a few news reporters who seemed to be looking for any type of emotion. At last, his family entered.

The moment I laid eyes on his mother, my heart began to fill with rage. She was a county employee in the same prosecutor's office I was in days before. I didn't want to see this demon-monster being provided with any special treatment. The prosecutor was aware of the situation but felt there was no need for us to worry. I disagreed, after all she was employed by the prosecutor's office as a victim's advocate. I watched as she paraded up and down the narrow hallway with a cup of coffee in her had, carefree and un-alarmed. This fed my anger. My brother called out to her to ask her name and confirm her identity.

After she disclosed who she was, she turned to me with little emotion and said, "I'm sorry for your loss." At that point I exploded. I jumped up in anger and yelled, "Are you the one who gave birth to that demon?" The prosecutor came down the stairs just then. He saw what was going on and rushed over. He approached one of the other advocates and said, "What is she doing here?" He ordered the advocate to take her from the building through a private entrance. He looked over to me and said, "it's time," as he entered a door to the judge's chambers.

The courtroom where our case was to be heard was very small. It looked nothing like the ones you see on TV court cases. There was a judge's bench and a jury box, but in the middle of the room was a large table that the prosecutor and the defense had to share. About four feet away from that table, were ten tiny chairs for the family and public. Families from one side were forced to sit elbow to elbow with those from another. I sat in the front row with Kim. Nervous and anxious, I waited to see this demon-monster. I wanted no one to get in my way of seeing this evil. I also didn't want to have to look at his family grieve over him. He didn't deserve it.

The prosecutor was the first to come in. He took a seat at the table. With him was this big, burly detective who had been at my ex-wife's house that terrible morning. Last to come was the council for the defense. He and the prosecutor made no effort to speak to each other. The judge walked in through a door next to his bench. At that point, a gray haired gentleman yelled, "All rise!" As the judge made his way to the bench, the door quickly flew open again. Before we had a chance to be seated, a sheriff's deputy appeared. Right behind him, in shackles and cuffs, was the defendant. All of us remained standing to see this demon-monster that had killed my daughter. The gray haired gentleman, reminded us to have a seat but my legs were frozen. I stood there and stared at him. The prosecutor, the bailiff, and the judge kept asking me to take my seat, but I couldn't. With a smirk grin on his face, the defendant strolled over to the table where council was seated and nonchalantly took a seat where the deputy had pointed.

I stood there, frozen at the sight of this thing. Everyone in the courtroom became nervous, afraid of what I might do. Kim tried to pull me into my seat, but I couldn't move. This was no person, this was no human being. This was pure evil. He looked as if he had seaweed or dirty rags hanging off of him. His eyes told the story as if he were proud of what he had done. He didn't appear nervous or frightened, as I thought he would. He just grinned.

Still standing frozen in the courtroom, at 9:00 in the morning on January 24th, 2000; I came face to face with Satan himself. No one in this world could convince me otherwise.

I looked at his hands, the hands that had taken my daughter's life, and I lost control. I called him a "motherx!*xer and a s*n ofa bi*xh" as I leaped over the railing in front of me. Without hesitation, the prosecutor and a detective came over and grabbed me. They weren't able to move me. I was a stone. The next thing three sheriff's deputies that had been standing in the door were on me, pushing me to the floor with knees in my back holding me down, keeping me from that demon. I kept looking at the deputy's gun less than eight inches from my reach. I kept thinking to myself, if I took the gun, I could end this all right now. He had his back turned towards me, so it would've been easy to take it without him noticing. Before I could make a decision to act on my impulse, the deputies, prosecutor and the detective proceeded to drag me out of the courtroom. Once they had me in the hallway, they reentered the courtroom and locked the door behind them.

Kim stayed inside, pleading mercy for me. I could hear her voice clearly as I stood in the hallway. Before they threw her out, she managed to hear that the hearing and trial had been postponed until the last week in June. The defense attorney had apparently made an argument over some DNA evidence, so the Judge allowed him time to prepare some research. The hearing was supposed to be a step in the process but it amounted to nothing. Kim and I waited in the hallway for about twenty minutes, in hopes of learning about any new information that could act in our favor.

The Sheriff's deputies were ready to bring the prisoner out of the courtroom. The hearing had ended. They were to bring him through the same hallway where I was standing. One of the deputies came over to me and angrily said, "I want you outside!" I quietly obeyed him. He escorted me to an exit door at the end of the hall. I turned to stare out of the little window in the center of the door, as he shut it behind me. I stood there and watched. I saw them escort that "demon-thing" into a room off to the side, which I later found out was the holding cell. I could hear the chains that shackled his feet, as they clanked across the floor. Helpless in any way, I just stood there.

Once the hall was cleared, the deputy released me. As he opened the big steel door, the man who had been mean and angry shed a tear. He turned to me and said, "I want him just as much as you do, along with the rest of my guys. But, the law says until he goes to trial we have to protect him." He'll get his!" he said as he turned and walked away.

I drove home that day with a sense of fear from what I had witnessed. I was also disappointed in myself for

losing my cool in the courtroom. I thought I was prepared.
I didn't want to take any more chances and mess things up.
I hoped I hadn't. Kim kept asking me if I was OK? I said,
"Yeah, I'm fine." I didn't want to tell her about what I had
seen. I would tell no one. Who would believe me anyway.
I knew whom I had seen.

5
Arizona Trip

It was late February and Kim had long since gone back to work, as had the rest of my family. The kids were in school and I left alone to pace around the house and think about Virginia. Everyone, I thought, had returned to his or her life, everyone except me.

I would look out and see everything covered with snow. The freezing temperatures had sent everyone and everything to take cover and hide. I felt as if I was left with nothing and I had no one. My activities were limited because of the weather, and I was left with no choice but to stay indoors, alone, and grieve.

Everyday was a replay of the day before. I would get up from bed and go directly to the front room and lie on the sofa. I would pace, from time to time, only to stop and gaze at the pictures of my daughter on the wall. With each passing day I became more despondent and sank deeper into my depression. I didn't know what to think anymore and I didn't know what to do. I began to let the notion of suicide enter my head. The thought of dying didn't scare me. If anything, it gave me a feeling of relief to know I would see my baby again, but for the sake of the others, and for my own sake, I had to figure out another way.

That same day when Kim came home from work, I asked her what she thought about moving away. I figured, if I put enough distance between the painful surroundings and me, I could find peace and make a fresh start somewhere else. I knew Kim would agree with anything that would bring me some happiness, so we began to make plans to move out west, and in preparation made plans to take a trip to Arizona. I've heard many good things about living there, so I thought it would be a perfect place for us to make a fresh start. I called my brother and told him to pack a bag. I hoped that by going, I could escape the daily torture I was facing in that house, and at the same time I would prepare the family for the big move. I felt that this was the only alternative to suicide, the thought of which was becoming more appealing to me every day.

When my brother and I began our trip to the west, we also began a journey to our own childhood. We recalled the days we played little league baseball at Fulton Road Park.

We would get up early in the morning, put our uniforms on and head for the park. We would play catch until the rest of the team arrived. My brother was the catcher, so I would always call him Yogi Bera. I was always in the outfield where the chances of catching a ball and having to throw it to the infield were slim to none. It didn't matter, I was part of a team, and that was good enough for me.

One day, purely by accident, I swung the bat and connected with the ball. It went soaring through the air. I stood there watching and admiring it as it landed past the centerfield. Suddenly, I became aware of my team, the coach and the crowd yelling and shouting at me to run. I barely made it to first base. The first base coach snarled at me angrily and asked why I wouldn't run. I smiled and waved at my brother. Now I could be called Roger Maris, or Mickey Mantle.

We continued our journey to the past when during the winter months we would bundle up and take our make shift sleds to the snow-covered hill at Oakwood Park. We would struggle to climb that hill to feel the exhilaration of sliding back down and finally tumbling into the snow. We would spend hours on that hill, until we got too cold and wet. We would walk home shivering, with smiles on our faces.

I leaned back in my seat to think about my childhood. It was a time in my life when I wasn't aware of the tragedy and evil that existed in the world. It was a time when I didn't know that hearts could break, or that tears could flow from your eyes in an endless stream of pain. I didn't know that grief and sorrow could follow you around like old friends, even on a three thousand mile trip to the west. I cried when I realized that through the years, a little piece at a time, I had lost the innocence of my youth. I was now a guilty old man, guilty of knowing the pain of having lost a child.

In a silent gesture of comfort, my brother placed his hand on mine as we drove under the arch through "The Gateway to the West".

After three days of a very tiresome road trip, we arrived in Avondale, Arizona a small city south of Phoenix. We found a Comfort Inn for the night so we could be rested and ready to go out and stake my claim the following morning. I looked out to watch the sun go down over the mountains, and for a brief moment, I thought I had found the paradise I was so desperately searching. I laid down that night, a little homesick, with sweet thoughts of Virginia on my mind. I said a prayer as I closed my eyes.

Morning came quickly. I opened my eyes to the bright sun and the first thing I noticed was that Kim wasn't there with my coffee so I went to the coffee shop. It was a gorgeous day, but I didn't feel exhilarated like I'd hope. I decided that after my coffee, I would look around town at some of the real estate and at some potential job sites for Kim.

We showered and shaved to prepare for a day of driving around town, searching for the unexpected. We drove up and down the streets of Avondale looking at houses for sale. I was expecting to find a special house, a house that would say "Here is where you'll find peace and comfort."

I hoped maybe something or someone would find me and change the way I felt. Every now and then my brother would point to a house he thought would appeal to me. I'd only shrug my shoulders and shake my head in disapproval. We continued the search until we got tired of driving and sweating from the Arizona heat.

We returned to our room to shower and change our clothes. We decided to go to the hotel bar and have a few drinks before turning in for the night. Tomorrow we would begin our search again, perhaps on the other side of town.

Early the next morning, we drove to the eastside of Avondale, only to find a run down neighborhood. The houses were dilapidated and in need of major repairs. The lawns were filled with trash and old tires. There was no need to look there, so we quickly left that neighborhood and drove to Goodyear, a city near Avondale.

Again we drove up and down the streets looking for that Garden of Eden. As the day wore on, I slowly began to realize that there was no such place. My brother must have noticed the look of dismay on my face and suggested we return to our room.

We went back to the hotel and sat by the pool. While my brother drank his beer, I wondered where and when I would find peace and comfort again. I knew my search in Arizona was over. Even though it was a beautiful state, with snow-capped mountains in the distance and the cacti reaching toward the sky, I began to feel homesick. I missed Kim and the kids. I missed the city I called home.

As the sun began to set, we went to the hotel bar and had a couple of drinks. I found out first hand that sedatives and alcohol do not mix well at all. I reached for my brother's arm and asked him to help me to the room. With my brothers help, I staggered down the hallway. A gentleman approached us and before he said I word I shouted at him, "Get the fxxk out of my way, can't you see I'm coming through!"

After struggling to open the door, my brother managed to lead me to the bed. I sat there weaving from side to side trying to regain some balance. I assured my brother that I was fine, so he went to take a shower. As I waited my turn, I began to cry when I realized that no matter how far you travel and no matter where you go, the baggage of pain and grief follows you. There was no Garden of Eden in Arizona or Ohio, not anywhere.

My brother came out of the shower to find me sitting on the bed crying. He didn't say a word. He sat next to me and put his arm around me. He allowed me to cry until I was empty. In a drunken stupor, I laid on the bed and fell fast asleep.

The next morning we packed our luggage and began the long trip home. For hours we drove in silence. I tried to enjoy some of the beauty of this country. I was sure that I wouldn't pass this way again.

As I pulled down the sun visor, I saw the picture of my daughter, which she had placed there when I bought the truck. As the memories flooded my head I could almost hear her say, "This is so we'll always be together daddy." I though about Virginia and what that son of bxxch monster had done to her. I wondered if he had any idea what he had done to my family and to me.

I knew that once I got home, I would have to deal with the trial and all the aggravation would come with it. I also knew I would have to battle with my depression, my pain and my grief. At the time I didn't know how.

As I got closer to Ohio, the cold, gray weather I had tried to escape intensified the feelings I had within. I wanted to go to bed. In my desperation, suicide seemed to be my only way out. There would be no more pain. I began to make plans as to how I would take my own life.

We finally made it home to Ohio. I walked into an empty house. Kim was at work and the kids were in school. I went directly to my daughter's picture and kissed it. I thought about all the different ways I could kill myself. I settled on shooting myself in the head. I imagined it would be quick and almost painless. There would be no chance that I would be saved. It was done. I knew what I wanted to do. A feeling of relief came over my mind. I knew now that my pain would end forever. Exhausted from the long drive home, I fell asleep on the sofa, holding the picture of my little girl.

6

The Hospital

Part I

Tomorrow morning I thought, when Kim was at work and the kids were at school, I would take a gun, drive to an isolated place and end it all. I didn't want Kim to have to come home and see me. I was just as dead anyway. I had quit showering and shaving. Every morning I put on the same clothes and wore them for weeks. I would stay in bed or sit on the sofa, just staring at the ceiling or floor. I was a basket case, a burden to Kim and the kids. I sat and cried thinking I'd never see my child again. But tomorrow, all that would change. I was relieved by my decision.

I didn't know that Kim would derail my plans that evening. She came home from work that night and she knew something was not right. When she talked to me she was a little edgy. I could hear fear and nervousness in her voice. Maybe she had other things on her mind I thought, but she looked at me from time to time as if she could see into my mind. As if she saw the gun to my head.

She made dinner for the kids and helped them with their homework. After she showered the kids and put them to sleep, I thought she would go to bed and leave me to finish planning my fate. However, Kim came over and sat beside me. She knew something was wrong. She took my hand and began to convince me that I needed help.

"You can't go on like this!" she said. "There's medicine, therapy, and people who can help you through this, please!" She began begging me to allow her to take me to the hospital. I couldn't, I thought to myself, because of what I had planned for the next morning. Kim got down on her hands and knees before me. I looked at her crying and I reluctantly agreed.

"Maybe, you're right," I said. I couldn't bear to see her cry. The moment I said yes, she packed me a bag and before I could change my mind, she led me out of the door and off to the hospital.

I hated hospitals and even worse I hated emergency rooms, but it was in the emergency room where we had to begin the admittance process. Instead of waiting. Kim convinced a cleaning lady and a nurse to sneak me through a rear entrance and usher me into an examining room. She knew that if I were kept waiting I would leave and she'd have no chance of saving me. Once inside, we waited for an intake nurse from the psychiatric unit to assess me. The wait was a little long, but I had no chance to escape. Kim made them aware of my ordeal so they placed me in a locked room. A short time later, the nurse arrived. She took one look at me and said, "We're going to help you here, honey, come with me please." I must have looked horrible for her to say this to me before even assessing me.

She took us from the room and led us down a long hallway. We stopped in front of a set of elevators. My knees began to shake. This was becoming too real for me, and I wanted to back out. We stepped inside the elevator that took us to the second floor. We stepped out right in front of the double-door entrance to the psychiatric unit. I was hesitant to walk through those doors because I didn't know what to expect. I was scared but I had no choice. I looked to Kim and saw a sense of relief in her eyes.

It was late and most of the ward was dark. The lights were turned off except for a bank of lights over the nurse's station. A nurse came over and took the bag that Kim had prepared for me. She dumped it out onto the counter, taking everything she thought I could use to hurt myself. I was taken to a small room to wait for a doctor. A minute later, a small man in a black suit and tie came in and sat beside me. He began to ask questions about my daughter, if we were close. I was without words. Kim was quick to answer. He patted me on the back and asked a nurse to take me to put away the few items I was allowed to keep.

The hospital room wasn't what I had expected. I thought I would walk into a room covered in rubber walls with a mat on the floor. Instead, it looked like a normal hospital room. There was a reclining hospital bed with a small dresser beside it. In the comer was a lounge chair facing the window. The only thing unusual was the thick, steel security screen that covered the window that made me feel as if I were caged.

Kim was soon asked to leave, but I didn't want her to go. I knew that once she left, I would be alone in a strange place among strangers. She hugged me and reassured me that everything was going to be fine. I kissed her good-bye and she turned to leave, closing the door behind her.

Suddenly, I was all alone in a dark room. I felt like a failure. I had lost my daughter and I couldn't cope. I battled depression and I lost. I sat in the chair with my head down and began to cry as I thought about my daughter and where I had ended up. I tried to muffle the sounds of my crying so no one would hear me. I didn't want to discuss my defeat with anyone. I just wanted to be left alone.

My crying left me exhausted. I walked to the bed and lay there, fully clothed with my baseball cap on. I slipped off my shoes and within minutes, I fell asleep.

Morning arrived and for a moment, I forgot where I was. I looked towards the light shining in my room and the security screen on the window quickly reminded me where I was and how I got there. I put on my slippers and ventured out into the ward. No one said anything to me as to what to do or where I was supposed to be, so I began to wander and look around. I started at the nurse's station and began walking down the hallway that formed a big circle around the ward. Most of the rooms were for patients. Every once in a while, I'd see one marked laundry, group therapy, recreational therapy, or shower room. I saw a room marked patient lounge. It had a TV and some lounge chairs in it. Before I knew it, I was back at the nurse's station. I had walked in one big circle and ended up nowhere.

There was one room in particular that caught my eye. I saw some patients sitting in there smoking, so I thought I'd join them. It was a very small room with a handful of chairs. There was a brown box mounted on the wall, which I found out was the lighter. There were no lighters allowed on the psych ward.

I sat beside a woman and she immediately introduced herself as Nelie. She was a black lady, kind of short and stocky. She held a cigarette in one hand and a hairbrush in the other. Across from where we sat was a tall, black man who introduced himself as Thomas. I spoke my name, then we sat in silence smoking our cigarettes.

A short while later, a nurse walked in and asked who I was. When I said my name, she told me that my doctor was here and he wanted to seem me. I followed her out of the smoke room to a small office behind the nurse's station where he was waiting for me.

"How are you feeling today?" He asked. I shrugged my shoulders and said, "OK. I guess." He proceeded to ask me a few other questions, but his thick accent made it hard for me to understand, so I shrugged my shoulders again.

He wrote notes continuously, looking at me once in a while. When he finished writing, he turned to me and told me that he was prescribing some medication for me so that I would feel better; an antidepressant, and antipsychotic and a sleeping pill. He closed his notebook and said, "You can go now." I think he was from the Philippines. I couldn't understand most of what he said. He was very professional looking. I hoped he knew what he was doing. I left to return to the smoking room. As soon as I lit up, a call came over the P.A. system announcing that group therapy was about to begin. Everyone began to leave the smoke room, so I followed behind them.

We filed into the room marked group therapy and took a seat. The chairs had been arranged in a circle. Nelie and Thomas were there. I noticed that there were a couple of kids there too. They couldn't have been more than sixteen or seventeen years old at the most. I sat and looked at them and wondered why they were there. There was an older gentleman too. He was dressed in what appeared to be a dark blue uniform of some sort. He was bald and looked as if he'd spent his whole life working in a factory.

A rather large lady wearing a blue smock began the session by asking us to state, on a scale from 1 to 10, how we felt and why? Nelie went first. "Today," she said, "I feel like a five. I woke up today feeling pretty good." She added.

I noticed she still held the hairbrush in her hand. Thomas went next. He said he felt like a five too. He had talked to his kids that morning and was feeling pretty good about it. The group continued around the circle until it was my turn. "I just got here, and I feel like a zero." I said. That was the end of my first group therapy session.

It took a while to get around the circle, and it was time for lunch. It was also visitation time. I walked out of her therapy room and Kim was standing there. She and I had lunch together. I was happy to see her. I told her that I didn't like it and that I wanted to go home.

"Give it a chance!" She said. "You haven't even been here a full day, yet!" We sat and talked. Before we knew it, visitation had ended it was time to walk Kim to the door.

"I'll be back this evening." She said. In a second, she was gone and I was alone again.

During the rest of the day, I went to a relaxation therapy session. The therapist taught us ways to relax when we became anxious. Afterwards, we attended a recreational therapy class until it was time for dinner. Some of us drew pictures while other made trinkets out of wood. I decided to make a jewelry box for Kim. It was something to keep my mind busy.

It was getting time for visitation and dinner. I was looking forward to seeing Kim again. I was waiting by the door when she came in. She had bought me something to eat, so we went to my room. I asked how the kids were doing.

"Everything is fine." She said. She told me not to worry about anything. We sat there in the privacy of my room and talked about all that we had been through and how I missed my daughter. Visitations were kept short, and soon, Kim had to leave again.

That evening I was given a sleeping pill. Not knowing the effect it would have on me, I went to the smoking room to have a cigarette. Within a few seconds, I had to butt my cigarette and stagger to my room. I flopped on the bed and quickly fell asleep.

The next morning, I awoke to find that I still had my clothes and shoes on. I decided to shower, shave, and change my clothes. I ate my breakfast in a hurry. I wanted to smoke a cigarette before group therapy began. In order to be released, group therapy was mandatory.

This time the therapy session began a little differently. The therapist wanted everyone to make a brief statement as to what had brought them there.

Nelie went first again. She told the story of how she had lived with her mother for years and how one day, she came to find that her mother had died of natural causes. Nelie became very depressed then and lived in a state of confusion. She held up the hairbrush. "This belonged to my mother," she said, "Her hair is still in it."

Next it was Thomas' turn. His story was totally different. Thomas had been sent there by court order. He had a history of drug and alcohol abuse. He'd been in an accident and a passenger had been seriously hurt. This wasn't the first time that this had happened or was this his first visit here. He had been in jail for some other problem. To look at Thomas, you' d never know he had a drug problem. He spoke softly and eloquently. You could tell by his choice of words that he was an educated man. I later came to know that Thomas was very knowledgeable about the Bible. He would often make references to specific chapters and verses that were his favorites.

The two young girls had been placed there by their parents. For reasons they didn't disclose, they had become unruly and out of control in school and at home. One of them stood up and showed the group her wrist, proudly displaying a mark where she had cut herself. A feeble attempt at suicide, I thought. It looked more like a cry for help or sympathy. She'd been heard, all right, because she was with the rest of us, crying for help.

When it was my turn I only managed to say that I was suffering from depression, nothing else. I couldn't bring myself to discuss my story, not yet.

As the days went by, I began to feel a little better. My medication had taken effect. In group therapy I began to discuss the reason I was there. They had all read about it in the newspapers and watched the story on the TV news. Everyone seemed to have a special sympathy for me. Even the nurses went out of their way and made special exceptions for me. They knew I wasn't mad, just sad.

Nelie, Thomas and I became well acquainted.

We would often meet in the smoke room and discuss our problems. There in the smoking room, we held a different kind of therapy. It was more personal, more revealing, and it seemed to work for me better than the regular groups.

One evening, Kim's pastor came to visit me, but it wasn't just a visit. She brought me a revelation. In the privacy of my room, she began to reveal to me that the hand of God had awakened her. She had been shown a vision of my daughter in the moment of terror, but before she suffered, she cried for God and He had come to rescue her from the hand of that monster. I had always prayed that God would take care of my children, and He hadn't let me down. He had sent this pastor to tell me so. I thanked her for bringing me her message. She stood up to leave. I asked her to stay, but she insisted she had to leave. She said a prayer with me and left. I watched her as she left my room that day. She was a woman of the Word of God, and you could see in her eyes a glow of happiness and contentment I had never seen before.

I had spent many sleepless nights anguishing over how my daughter had died and the terror of what she had gone through, but that day through a messenger from God, I laid it to rest.

The following afternoon I had another visitor. This time, it was the pastor from my old church who had spoken at my daughter's funeral. I hoped he was bringing me another message. He was a tall, young man with a peaceful look about him. I began to wonder if all pastors had that glow. He greeted me by my door and we grabbed a couple of chairs and sat down. He sat directly across from me.

I began to confess to him those feelings of hatred and anger I was holding inside of me. These feelings were not only towards the man who killed my daughter, but also toward everything that had happened and everyone involved. He leaned toward me and said, "It's because you have yet to forgive..." Forgive? I thought. I'd never forgive those animals that had taken my daughter from me. In a gentle but persistent way, he began to tell me that as long as I harbored hatred and anger within me, there would never be room for anything else. There would be no room for joy or happiness, and especially no room for the Holy Spirit to bring me peace and guidance.

I had learned about forgiveness before. I had even read it in the Bible: "Forgive us our trespasses, as we forgive those who have trespassed against us..." This forgiveness my pastor was asking me to give was a tall order. I asked him to lead me in a prayer of forgiveness. We stood up and began to pray. There in my hospital room and in the presence of God I began to forgive the man who had killed my daughter.

I hugged him and thanked him for his prayers. He left me that afternoon with a gift; the knowledge that I had the ability to forgive. Nothing magical or miraculous happened, but I began to feel a sense of relief, a sense of peace I so desperately needed.

I walked down the hallway after the pastor left. I decided to join Nelie and Thomas in the smoking room. It was Nelie who spoke the words I so desperately want to hear.

"You look like you're ready to go home!"

Thomas patted me on the back and said, "I'm ready to go home myself!" I just smiled and said, "Yeah. I think I'm ready."

Kim was there at five as usual. She looked extra nice. She wore a black suit, had her hair done real nice, and wore a touch of perfume that she knew I liked. We walked to my room for privacy. She told me that she had news for me. A hearing has been set for the juvenile who was involved in our case. Kim, knew that it was tearing me up inside knowing that his accomplice was running the streets as if nothing happened, but his day of reckoning was soon at hand. It was only a week away.

It was late, already, and my doctor still hadn't come in. I figured it was too late for rounds, so I went to have my final cigarette before going to bed. At ten that night, the doctor showed up and called me to his office. I was tired and ready for bed. I wasn't up for a counseling session so late at night. When I walked in, I noticed he had a cheerful look on his face. To my surprise, he asked me if I was ready to go home? I said, "Sure? I thought he meant in the morning, but then he said, "You can go get your stuff now if you like?" I jumped out of my seat and shook his hand, thanking him over and over for all of his help. I went to the phone and immediately called Kim.

"Come get me, I'm being discharged!" I yelled. I hung up the phone before she had a chance to say anything.

I went to my room and quickly packed my belongings. While I waited for Kim to come rescue me. I looked for Thomas to say good-bye. To my disappointment, I learned from one of the nurses that Thomas had been discharged while I was in talking to the doctor. So I went to look for Nelie. I had to say good-bye to her too. I found her in the smokeroom. She was sitting there, all alone. She was holding a cigarette in one hand and the hairbrush in the other. I couldn't bring myself to go in and disturb her, so I silently said, "Good-bye, Nelie… I'll pray that you'll get well."

Kim had already been waiting for me by the door, I went directly to her. We looked toward the nurse's station so that someone could buzz us out. They were all waving and wishing us well as we walked out.

I left the hospital that night armed with medicine, some knowledge about depression, and some new coping skills. I also left knowing that I had the ability to forgive and that God didn't allow my child to suffer. Most importantly, I left with a glimmer of hope that I would make it.

When we got home that night, Kim and I took down my daughter's picture that was hanging in the living room. I held one of them close to me and whispered to Virginia in my mind, "I'm going to make it." I am going to make it for you and for me. I was going to make it for us.

Before Kim and I went to bed, I gave her the heart-shaped wooden jewelry box I had made in recreational therapy. She carried it to bed with her and placed it on the nightstand before she turned out the lights. To this day, it sits there next to her.

7

The Demon's Accomplice

On March 15th the juvenile who had been involved in my daughter's death, would finally answer to the courts.

Police investigations revealed that someone had seen one juvenile with the defendant the evening of the murder. The police quickly arrested him. After failing three voice stress tests, he began to confess to his role in the crime.

The parents of the juvenile brought in a lawyer for him. The defense lawyer advised the juvenile not to say another word in the interrogation process. The police knew that he wasn't the one who actually committed the crime, but they needed every bit of information from this kid to nail his partner.

The prosecutor and the defense attorney met and reached a plea bargain. The defense attorney made sure that this delinquent kept his mouth shut. He knew that his client had the information the police and the prosecutors wanted and desperately needed to get his client. The defense attorney also knew that he could get his client the minimal punishment with this information. With this leverage, the defense attorney convinced the prosecutor's office to enter a plea bargain in exchange for one count of tampering with evidence. For this, the juvenile would have to testify, in open court, to everything he had seen and participated. He would be tried as a juvenile and be released into the custody of his father until he answered to the courts. Today was that day.

For months, the fact that he was free gnawed at me to no end, but there was nothing I could do. An ignorant incompetent juvenile judge had set an accomplish to a murder free with the help of the prosecutor's office.

Since the day we found out that this kid had been released into his father's custody to await his fate, Kim and I had called the juvenile courts on a weekly basis. We wanted a court date set for him as soon as possible, to get him behind bars where he belonged. We were routed from one office to another. Most often we would be force to leave messages on voice mails, and no one would return our calls. There was always one excuse after another. People were suddenly taking numerous vacations or getting sick. We continued to call but got no reply.

When I became hospitalized, Kim had attempted to call everyone she could think of to get the monster's accomplice locked up, or least, get us a court date. She knew that at least knowing a date might help me in my recovery process. It would remove that gnawing anger inside of me that was controlling the depression within.

Out of desperation, Kim finally called a newspaper reporter who was willing to write an article about the struggle we were having over this juvenile demon. She was determined to get his court date set before the other defendant so that he could not avoid jail time for his aid and abetting. The news reporter wrote down everything Kim said.

The next day, the article appeared on the front page of the newspaper. It blasted the judge for her hasty decision. The article revealed the rude and insensitive treatment we had received from the juvenile prosector's office. We made threats and accusations towards every political person involved, and the reporter made sure to quote every word in the article. The article blasted the juvenile system as a whole. It also displayed the outrage that the entire community had for that particular judge and her decision to allow this demon-kid to be free.

Kim's plan had worked. Two hours after the newspaper hit the stands, she got the call we had been waiting for all this time. The juvenile prosecutor herself called to tell Kim that the hearing was set for March 15, 2000 and that was the best she could do. But Kim didn't let her off so easy. Kim let her know that the negligence displayed by her and her office was inexcusable. It was the two months of not knowing anything that had put me in my state of mind. She made it clear to the prosecutor that if her office could get a court date in a matter of a few hours that it should have been done months ago. Kim laid the blame of my breakdown on the prosecutor and informed her that if there were anymore mistakes, she would continue to use the media to seek justice.

It was a plan that proved successful, but Kim's plan was not complete. The community had to become involved. We knew there was strength in numbers. Kim had to insure that she could follow through on her threats. We decided that petitions would be our weapon.

Kim and I worked tirelessly and endlessly canvassing the neighborhood. We went to as many houses, businesses, and organized groups as we could, summoning signatures and letters to add to our petition. She took the petition to work, the grocery store, and even the gas station, anywhere she went the petition went with her. We gathered hundreds of names. People began to line up everywhere we went to sign the petition.

Many members of the community made it clear that this criminal was not wanted in our neighborhoods or on our streets. It was victory in our favor, but clearly it wasn't enough. We compiled hundreds of signatures, but needed more to prove to the judge that we were not going to rest until justice was served. We recruited the help of an organization called Parents of Murdered Children. In no time, the organization had compiled thousands of signatures nationwide. We knew now that we had enough ammunition to walk into the courtroom and insure that justice would be served by the people who should have done it in the first place.

Fortunately, the media was misinformed as to the time and date the trial was to begin. Looking back, I can't but wonder if this was deliberate, after all the attention our article had gotten. Regardless, it was good for me. I hadn't been out of the hospital for very long and the last thing I could handle was another unnerving situation.

When Kim and I walked into the courtroom, we were armed and prepared with a huge package of petitions. On the top of the red binder that encased each page, was a full color picture of my daughter. I wanted the judge to see what a beautiful young lady this criminal had helped destroy. I thought if she had a face to put with the name, she would understand that my actions meant something. It was personal, not towards her but for the love of my daughter. I wanted her to see what they had taken away from me.

A slender, young lady with short hair approached us and introduced herself as the prosecutor. She looked very professional and anxious to get started. She told us that she was the one who would be trying our case. We handed her the package and the picture of my Munchkin. She looked at the picture intently, and then looked at me and said we are about ready to begin.

She pointed down a hallway to a set of doors, telling us that it was the courtroom. I noticed that the hallway, which led there was lined with sheriff's deputies. They were searching everyone who was entering the courtroom with metal detectors. We walked over to the court entrance. When it came my turn to enter the room, they not only waved that metal detector over my entire body, but I also had to turn my pockets inside out. The deputies then patted down every inch of me. I didn't think I posed that great a danger, but they were not taking any chances.

I made my way down the aisle and took a seat in the front row. I sat between Kim and the advocate. I turned to look at the defense table. There sat the juvenile demon who helped a murderer instead of helping my daughter.

Within minutes, the judge took the bench and asked the prosecutor to begin her case. She walked over to the judge's bench and handed her the package I'd brought. She was a petite, older woman with a stern face, an expression she wore throughout the entire proceedings.

As I listened to the young prosecutor present her opening argument, I came to realize that she had done her homework. She had gone to the high school the defendant and my daughter had attended. She had looked up all the records of all the misdeeds he had committed. This so-called youthful offender had constantly been suspended from school for fighting with the other students, as well as staff and faculty members. He had made unwanted sexual advances, not only toward students, but toward teachers as well. At one time, he had run a lighter up a girl's arm in a mock attempt to set her on fire. After committing this act, he went on to brag to other classmates that he had already killed a person and set her on fire. He would go on to brag about how he would do it again. This was the same unspeakable act that was committed against my daughter. To the prosecutor, it was an illustration of his lack of character, to me it was a confession.

She continued to tell of more incidents, but I quit listening. All I could do was focus my eyes on this young man. He sat there, holding his head down, as did his parents. They were ashamed, the defendant ashamed of his own violent acts.

The prosecutor ended her case, but not before urging the judge to impose the harshest prison sentence allowed.

"It is necessary!" She said.

The defense attorney came to a podium that sat on the far side of the room next to where we were sitting. He mumbled through a short speech that was barely audible. He went on to blame society and the parents for the person that this defendant had become. He blamed the educational system, saying that it was due to its negligence that his client had become considered mildly retarded and incapable of making rational decisions. It was the fault of the media, his parent's separation, and his mother's drug addiction. It sounded like he was trying to even blame the judge. His speech was brief and then he ran out of words. It was the first time I'd ever seen an attorney at a loss for words. Not once had he blamed his client for any of his actions.

He was very short and very large for is height. His face was rosy red. With each word he spoke, it appeared as if he was struggling for every breath. He had gray hair and very big glasses. He stood at that podium with nothing to say. I think he knew all along there was nothing he could say in defense of what his client had already confessed to doing.

The judge became tired of hearing him ramble on about how ignorant and mentally challenged his client was. He repeated the same phrases five or six times. She told him she'd heard enough and told him to take his seat. The judge then asked if Virginia's mother or I had anything to say before she passed down the sentence. My ex-wife declined, but I had prepared a statement. I asked the prosecutor to read it on my behalf.

Basically in my written statement, I called the youth a coward. He had ample opportunity to help my daughter, but instead chose to help a murderer. His actions were just as horrible as the murder itself. The statement further read, that if your honor decided to set this accomplice free, on probation, she would be forcing me to take the law into my own hands. At hearing the statement "I would take the law into my own hands, "the stern-faced judge raised her eyebrows at me. I ended my statement by asking her to please look at my daughter's picture and decide where this yellow coward belonged. After the young lady prosecutor finished the statement, the juvenile judge nodded in my direction and thanked me for the statement.

Finally, the judge asked the defendant to rise to make any last statement before she passed sentence.

"I'm sorry I got hooked up wit' da dude."

He said. He never once looked in my direction. Never once did he say he was sorry for what had happened to my daughter. The judge told him to remain standing.

Before the judge began to speak, the boy's father rose from his chair and began pleading to the judge to allow him to take his son to a relative's house instead of an institution. He stood there making pleas of how he was going to do the things for his son that he failed to do in the past. The judge saw this act as insincere and in so many words let this man know that it was too little, too late.

"I can't see any reason why keeping you at home or in school would benefit you..." she said. "You have not availed yourself of any intervention in the past and I see no reason where you would do so in the future. Therefore, this court remands you to the custody of the Department of Youth Services until the age of 21."

I slumped in my seat, in relief, knowing that justice had finally been served. It wasn't the sentence I had hoped for, but I got great satisfaction knowing that he was now off the streets. Kim put her arms around me and my advocate hugged me as well. It was over. The judge looked at Kim and me with that stern look on her face, as if to say, "I know you were responsible for that article in the newspaper." I stared right back, as if to reply, "That's right, we're the ones that made you do the right thing." She quickly disappeared through a side door and into her chambers.

I stood there and watched as the deputies handcuffed the boy and took him away. I felt that he was a big oaf who had been "caught up" in a crime well over his head. Trying to appear tough put him behind bars. He could have just as easily been a hero if he would have helped my daughter, but it was too late. He was on his way to a life of misery in a correctional institution.

8
Reaquainted with Grief
Part II

As the days and weeks passed, I began to feel better. The medication continued to work and I thought I was returning to some type of normalcy.

I attended church every Sunday. I became active in discipleship meetings the pastor held every Wednesday and every day I cleaned the house for Kim. I even did the dishes and laundry. I managed to go to the golf range everyday to practice for the upcoming golf season. Everything, I thought, seemed to be going well.

I was trying to keep busy enough to erase the memory of those pictures the detective had shown me and, especially, the memory of the day I had to go to the morgue. Even though I tried to keep as busy as I could, I still found myself at times, looking out of the front room window, hoping to see my little girl walking up the driveway. The pain of having lost my child was still there, but I was trying to cope with it as best as I could. Deep inside, I knew that the pain would never go away.

Roy became my constant companion. He would come over every day just to keep me company. He'd always help me around the house doing yard work and such. He was a character all by himself. He combed his hair straight back into a ponytail. He wore a bushy mustache that hung down his jaw and he had a potbelly from all the beer he loved to drink. His eyes, however, were criminal looking. I remember joking with him once. I told him that those eyes, belonged on a picture in a post office somewhere next to the ten most wanted list. He laughed and said, "Yeah, right beside yours!"

Everything I thought was going well. By mid-June, I began to notice some strange, familiar feelings starting to resurface, the strange feeling in my knees, and a sense of anxiety and confusion.

At first, I though it was because the trial date was approaching, so I tried to shake the feeling off. I thought that those feelings would go away once the trial was over. Even Kim and Roy noticed the change and kept asking me if I was okay. I assured them that I was fine. I was just nervous about going to trial.

On June 20th, Kim and I found ourselves sitting in the basement courtroom waiting for the trial to begin. The prosecutor walked in and took a seat at the square table in the middle of the courtroom. He was followed by the defense attorney who did the same. Minutes later, a deputy escorted the defendant into the courtroom. Handcuffed and shackled, he took a seat next to his attorney. This time, he didn't have that stupid grin on his face, or that evil look like the last time I saw him. He looked nervous and frightened. I could hear the chains making noise as he fidgeted in his chair.

I looked at his hands again, wondering why and how he had taken my daughter's life. This time, I kept my mouth shut. I sat there quietly, in hopes that they would not drag me out of the court room again.

The prosecutor began by asking the judge to allow new evidence that had been discovered to be introduced. The defense attorney stood up to object. An argument ensued between them. They argued and yelled like two children in a playground arguing over a toy. The inexperienced judge just sat there, not knowing what to do.

The defense attorney then asked for a postponement in order to study this new evidence. The judge granted him the delay. The prosecutor threw his hands up in disgust and everyone began to walk out, including Kim and I. This wasn't going to be a trial at all. It was just another step in the process of the legal system.

I went home, disgusted at the ridiculous display of stupidity and immaturity I had witnessed. Now we would have to wait until August 23rd. It was not that far away, I thought, but I wondered if the trial would truly be held then, or if there was going to be another hearing with more disappointments.

Meanwhile, I began to feel the depression taking over again. I quit attending church and the discipleship meetings I had needed for spiritual uplifting. I quit everything, even showering an shaving and changing my clothes again. Once again I fell into the cave of depression I had so desperately fought to get out of before. I hid in my room most of the time. I wouldn't answer the door or the phone. I didn't want to see or hear anything from anybody. I was tired of it all. I was tired of living.

On July 8th, I woke to another early morning call. Kim walked into the bedroom and handed me the phone. She stayed to listen so I knew something was wrong. It was my brother calling. I could tell he was crying. "What's wrong?" "What happened?" He told me that our friend Roy had died. He was forty-six. Apparently he had been at a local bar having a couple of beers and decided to walk home. Minutes from his home, he collapsed and died of a heart attack. By the time the rescue squad arrived, he was already gone.

The cloud of depression that had been hanging over my head descended on me with full force. I laid in bed, staring at nothing, looking into space, wondering what was happening to my life. I knew I would have to summon every bit of courage to go to the funeral. I had to say good-bye to my oldest and dearest friend.

The funeral services were held for Roy on a Monday. It took everything I had within me to go to the funeral home, but Kim helped me walk over to the casket, to say good-bye to my best friend. His hair was styled in the ponytail fashion he always wore. I saw his big, bushy mustache, that became his trademark, but the eyes I had poked fun at were now tightly closed. I bent over and hugged him.

"Good-by old friend, I'll see you soon I hope." I said.

Roy had chosen to be cremated, so there would not be a long procession to follow. He was not a churchgoer, so there would be no eulogy or singing. I said a quick condolence to his mother and hugged her. I couldn't take anymore. I had to go home.

At home I went immediately to bed and began to stare at nothing again. Reacquainted with grief, I placed a pillow over my face and began to cry. I had hit rock bottom, and now I could see no way out. I found myself in the same stupor I had experienced before, but this time it was worse. My hands were trembling and wouldn't stop. I had chest pains, and I couldn't sit still. I kept wondering how I could have been feeling so good, and then all of a sudden go back to square one.

I overheard Kim talking on the phone. She was making arrangements with my psychiatrist to have me admitted into the hospital again. When she approached me I didn't argue. This time, I was eager to go. I thought I would go into the hospital and return feeling well again. I would get better like the last time. She packed a bag for me and soon we were on our way to the psychiatric ward.

Before I knew it we were in the emergency room. Since my doctor had already called to admit me, our wait wasn't long. A nurse from the psychiatric unit came to take me upstairs.

This time things were different. There were only two other people in the ward; a tall, young man who stayed in the lounge watching TV and a lady in a wheelchair who stayed in her room and said nothing at all. I had the ward practically to myself.

I walked around that familiar circular hallway, stopping only to rest my head against the wall. I would stand there hoping that my mind would snap and I'd go off into a fantasy land in the deep recesses of my mind where nothing could hurt me anymore, a place where I would hear nothing, see nothing is where I wanted to go, but it didn't happen. I went into the smoking room, alone with my thoughts.

"So this is it," I thought, "In and out of psych wards for the rest of my life. Here's where my future lies."

Night came and I walked over to the nurse's station to request a sleeping pill. Luckily, the doctor had called in and ordered that I continue with my medicine until he saw me. I was given a sleeping pill. Within minutes, I staggered to my room and fell asleep.

When morning arrived, a nurse came to wake me up. The doctor was here and ready to see me. Still groggy and half asleep, I went to his office. I proceeded to tell him that the medicine he prescribed the last time had quit working. I told him that I was back in the same condition that I was in before. He explained to me that a relapse was common. He prescribed a new antidepressant for me, but he told me it would take at least 4 weeks to take effect. With that, he patted me on the back and told me I'd be fine soon, and not to worry.

I attended only two group therapy sessions this time. With only three people in attendance, they were short and sweet. I had heard it all before, so I learned nothing new. All other therapy had been cancelled because everyone had gone on vacation. I was left alone to wander that long, circular hallway.

Sometimes I'd pretend to be walking in the park with my little girl. I remember her holding my index finger as she learned to walk along beside me. She would get tired and begin to cry. I would lift her in my arms and continue to walk and she would fall asleep on my shoulder.

At times I would enter the smoking room and recall the conversation between Thomas, Nelie, and me. We began to call those meetings our personal group therapy.

Although I missed them, I was glad they were gone. It meant they were on their way to recovery and hopefully never return to the psychiatric ward to share in my walk along the circular hallway, or to hold group therapy in the smoking room.

I recalled the group therapy sessions and the heart wrenching tragic events I'd heard before. There were times I wanted to go to the patient crying as they told their story, to hold them and hug them; to let them know I knew and understood how they felt. I didn't do it because I was unsure of their reaction. Instead, I looked at them to let them know I was listening. I learned I still had the ability to feel compassion to anyone willing to take hold of it. In the smoking room, there was nothing but silence and a stream of smoke from my cigarette. I began to feel lonely and sad,

I began to cry as I thought about my daughter and my best friend, Roy.

A nurse came in and told me dinner was ready. I went to the dining area to find no one there, just me and a plate of something called food. It smelled like day old garbage and looked even worse. I began to form it into a mound of mush. I used my spoon to flick food across the room and heard it thunk as it fell to the floor. I continued this process until all the food was splattered on the tiled floor.

As I got up from the table, a cleaning lady walked in and saw the mess I'd made. The heavy-set older lady looked at the mess and then at me. She shook her head in disgust and pointed her mop at me. I thought she was going to strike me with her mop, but she didn't. She began to clean the mess. I assumed she was used to things like that, after all, it was a psychiatric ward.

I went back to the smoking room to wait for my sleeping pill. A short while later a nurse showed up with my medicine. I knew that soon my head would begin spinning and I'd stagger to my room and flop down on my bed and sleep.

This time the sleeping pill didn't work fast enough. I went to my room and sat in a big green chair next to the window. It began to rain. It was a soft and gentle rain making no sound as it fell on the window. From my window I could see the courtyard with two white benches facing each other.

I imagined the gentle rain were tears from heaven, tears from the angels above. Some of them were shedding tears of joy for they had a new angel in their midst. Some were tears of sorrow for the angel I had missed. We cried in unison. I yearned to be outside so our tears could mingle and soften my pain, and help to heal my broken heart. All I could do was helplessly watch the tears from heaven fall on the benches and onto the courtyard below.

I took the Bible from the nightstand and lay on the bed as if holding it alone would comfort me.

The tears from heaven began to fall harder. I could hear the tapping noise on the window. It sounded like a lullaby I'd heard before. A lullaby that put me to sleep clutching onto the Bible I held next to me.

The next morning the doctor was waiting for me in his office. I was surprised when he said I looked much better and could go home that afternoon.

This time after five days in the psychiatric ward the only thing I took home with me was a batch of new prescription forms. I left the hospital and stepped out into a hot July afternoon. On my way home I noticed the sun was shining, but not for me. I wondered if the sun would ever shine for me again.

9

Beginning My Recovery

I went home to pick up where I had left off. I either lay on the bed and stared at the ceiling or sat on the sofa and stared at the floor. Once in a while, I would look out the front room window. I still hoped to see my daughter walking up the driveway. It became a habit I didn't want to break.

One morning, however, things would start to change. I walked into the bathroom and caught a glimpse of myself in the mirror. I looked horrible. My hair was matted down on one side and sticking straight up on the other side. I had not shaved in days, almost weeks. My beard was scraggly looking. My eyes looked as if they were sunken in and I began to cry as I looked at what was happening to me.

I knew what I had to do. I had the knowledge and the skills to battle this depression. All I needed was the desire and the willingness to fight. I knew that God wasn't going to come to shave me or hand me a bar of soap and push me in the shower. These were steps I had to take for myself. I began to pray for the strength. I wiped the tears from my eyes and began to shave. It took almost an hour. I got in the bath and took a long hot shower, all the time praying for the strength to continue. I changed my clothes and went back to look at the man in the mirror. I vowed that day I would never look that horrible again.

I promised Virginia the same thing. I wasn't going to lie down and die. I wasn't only going to fight my depression, I was going to win. I made myself another promise. I swore that I was going to do something everyday, some task that would make me feel like I had accomplished something that day.

I began to clean the house, do laundry and the dishes. When Kim came home that afternoon she noticed the difference.

"It's about time!" She said. We both knew that this was the day I really began my recovery. I knew it was going to be a very long, hard struggle, but I also knew I was going to win. I thanked God for the strength that he had graciously given. To this day, I have held true to my promise to Virginia and that man in the mirror.

Each day afterward proved to be a struggle. It was difficult, but I continued to push myself and Kim helped on the really bad days. I became exhausted by the most menial task. Just when I thought I could do no more, Kim was there to push me on.

I began to think about Kim a lot. I saw how she had been there for me all along. Sometimes I thought maybe God knew I would be weathering this storm so He had sent Kim to me, to help me and be my companion. I felt as if I owed her so much. When she came home from work that night, I asked her to marry me. She was elated and quickly began to make calls, telling everyone the news and began making the arrangements.

We decided to get married on August 12th. The pastor who had delivered the eulogy for my daughter, would perform the wedding ceremony. I felt confident in her being the one God had chosen to marry us because Pastor Laurie was the one God had revealed the revelation about my daughter's rescue.

August 12th came quickly. Some friends and family gathered for the ceremony. Our children were there too. Kim had chose a long, ivory colored gown for the wedding. She looked beautiful, but most of all, she looked happy. I had not seen her this happy in months. The ceremony was short. Within minutes, Kim and I became husband and wife. In the back of my mind, I thought about Virginia and how happy she would have been on this day. She loved Kim and she would always ask us, "When are you guys going to get married, already?"

Kim's parents held a backyard reception for us. They had tables set up with Spanish, Mexican and Japanese food and liquor. I watched Kim as she made her way around to all the tables, greeting guests and sharing her joy with everyone. My sons were there and a couple of my brothers showed up. For the first time in over a year, I sat there, relaxed, watching Kim mingle. I imagined Roy sitting across from me, guzzling his beer.

Music started playing and people began dancing. I was glad to see everyone having such a good time, especially Kim. Everyone was having a good time, maybe too good because there were a couple who ended up getting sick and having to be taken home. It was getting late, and more people began to leave. Kim and I left late. Holding hands, we went home together as husband and wife.

The next day, I woke up to see a ring on my finger. I knew I had the ability to make plans and carry them out. I felt a since of new found hope. I had made a promise to Virginia and one to myself. Now, I had made a promise and a vow to Kim. Not only was I proving to be a fighter, I was also becoming a winner.

On August 23rd, another hearing was held and my wife and I found ourselves on the lower level of the courthouse the third time. This time, it was a little unusual. There was no prosecutor, no defense attorney and no defendant. We looked at each other with wonder, thinking maybe we had made a mistake and were here on the wrong date. We sat there, waiting for someone to make an appearance. Suddenly, screaming and yelling was coming from the judge's chambers. We stepped out into the hallway to see what was going on. We could hear the prosecutor, the defense attorney, and the judge arguing at the top of their lungs. There were insults and profanity being used by all of them. Their argument lasted twenty minutes. A news reporter stood by the door, frantically taking notes and writing down every word they said. The few people that were seated in the hall sat there and looked at each other with amazement and disbelief. It was very unprofessional and far worse than anything I had ever witnessed on TV.

A door flew open and the prosecutor hurried away. We got up to follow him when a victim's advocate from his office approached us and said the judge had failed to make a decision as to whether or not to allow the new evidence, so a jury trial was now scheduled for December 11th. As soon as I heard the date, I stormed up the steps and out of the courthouse with Kim rushing to catch up with me.

The tables had turned. This was no longer about my daughter. It was about the criminal and protecting his rights. I kept thinking, what about my daughter's rights? Where were they when she needed protection? I was angry and disappointed at the whole justice system.

I tried to put the fiasco out of my mind. I did not want to let those jerks impede my progress. I had learned one thing, no matter what happens, time marches on and December 11th would be here soon enough. I would continue to be true to my promises and vows until then.

Soon it was November 21st, a solemn day for me. Virginia would have turned sixteen years old that day. I spent the day recalling her 15th birthday, and how happy she had been. I would not be preparing her favorite meal this year or giving her a present. I remembered the videotape we made that year. I went into the bedroom closet and took it out. I stood there for a moment, holding it in my hand. I carried the tape into the front room, placed it in the VCR and began watching. I bent down and placed my hand on the front of the television as if to stroke Virginia's hair and touch her face. When I heard her voice, I could not contain myself. With my face on the TV screen, I began to cry.

November 23rd was even worse. It was the first anniversary of her death and it was also Thanksgiving Day. Kim parents invited us for dinner. I ate a little, mostly to appear polite, but all I really did was pick at the food. It was not a very happy day and could not find much for which to be thankful.

10
The Trial

The day I had been waiting on for over a year was finally here. I hoped it would be a quick trial and an even quicker sentencing. I was positive that the jury would render a guilty verdict.

When Kim and I arrived at the courthouse, it was jammed with newspaper reporters, television news people, and a slew of potential jurors. We could hardly make our way through the hallway that had become so familiar to us. The prosecutor and the lead detective on the case came over to greet us. "This is it!" They said. They seemed to be excited about the trial. They too had waited over a year to bring the monster to justice.

There was still some waiting. The jurors had to be chosen. Kim and I stepped outside to smoke a cigarette. On our way down the stairs, the defense attorney leaned over to me. Angry at the fact that he approached me, I shoved him against the wall with my shoulder and called him a maggot son-of-a-bxxxh. He ran down the stairs and directly to the prosecutor to complain about my behavior.

A short while later, the prosecutor emerged from the courtroom and summoned me to a corner of the hall. He asked about the incident that had taken place between me and the defense attorney. I confessed to shoving him and cursing at him. Before I had a chance to explain myself, he began screaming at me and scolding me like a child. He not only barred me from the courtroom, but also had me removed from the entire building. I would find out later why he wanted me removed from the building. I also learned that this particular attorney was known for pulling stunts like this with hopes of getting his guilty clients a mistrial. The prosecutor was not taking any chances of that happening with this case. He waited too long and worked too hard at building a conviction. He wanted this demon-monster in prison just as badly as I did.

I went home angry. I was angry with myself for having lost my cool. Angry at the fact that I allowed that defense attorney to lure me into his trap. Now, I thought, I'll never get the chance to defend my daughter. I won't be able to tell the world what a loving and beautiful child this demon had taken from me. At home, I could do nothing but sit and wonder what was going on. What was being said in the trial? Were we winning or were we losing? Did I cause a mistrial?

I paced around the house, anxious to hear any news, but none came. All I could do was wait on the morning paper and listen to the TV reports. The articles provided some information, which helped, but they were just as sketchy as my own imagination when it came to details.

It was already day two into the trial. I learned from the paper that the prosecutor had already called the coroner and some of the detectives to testify. The article stated that the autopsy report was read and some four-foot by two foot pictures of my daughter's mutilated body were displayed around the courtroom. I was grateful that I didn't have to see those awful photographs. On day two, character witnesses were to be brought in. I sat in disappointment, because I was supposed to be the lead character witness to speak for my daughter. The defense attorney knew this. He also knew the history of my hospital stays and breakdowns. He had seen me cry before, so he knew I would have a strong impact on the jury. I still believe this is why he pulled his dirty stunt.

By day three, Kim and I still had yet to receive a phone call about the status of our case. We watched the news and read the papers. The articles told about some of the different witnesses who testified, but little about their actual testimony. We were left totally in the dark. All we knew was that it hadn't been postponed again.

The paper announced the juvenile was scheduled to testify on day four of the trial. It would be his testimony that would ensure the prosecution of a conviction. We sat and paced around the house waiting for a phone call or any sort of update, but nothing came. I had given up all hope of having the opportunity to personally witness justice being served. I had no idea of what was being said or done in that courtroom. All I could do, at this point, was pray.

Friday, day five, arrived. We still didn't know, at this point, how long the trial was going to last. The newspaper said the defense was supposed to begin their presentation of the case. I also spoke about the testimony the juvenile had given the day before. The article included some gruesome details given by the witness. Reading it, Kim took that section of the paper and threw it in the trash. She would usually read every word to me, knowing I was anxious to know everything that was going on. This time, she refused.

I had a doctor's appointment scheduled for the same day. I looked forward to going, just so that I could get out of the house and distract my mind from thoughts about the trial. Kim and I got into my truck and left for the appointment.

When we got there, Kim was made to sit in the waiting room. I sat in the private office, talking about the trial with the doctor. The session became very intense. I began to cry. The suspense was getting the best of me. I opened up to this man and told him about all the feelings I was having about the trial. I had been holding back from Kim because I knew she was under enough stress already. I didn't want to burden her anymore.

Just as I was getting deep into the discussion, the office door flew open. Kim came rushing in waving her phone in her hand and yelling, "The jury's out! The jury's out!" I wiped the tears from my eyes and rushed out of the office. As we were walking out the office door, I learned that the noon news broadcast reported that the trial was over and the jury was in deliberation. I wanted to get home immediately to await any news about the verdict.

As we walked into the house, there was another news broadcast about the trial. The juvenile, who had been transformed from his correctional facility, was recalled to the stand. Again he gave a very graphic, detailed account of what had happened to my daughter on November 23rd. Graphic details I didn't want to hear. My wife had already hidden the newspaper and urged me not to watch the news. She was afraid that if I heard about what happened to my daughter, I would fall into a depression from which I would never return. She also feared that I would lose control again.

I agreed to turn the television off, but asked her to call the prosecutor for me. Now that the trial was over, I was hoping the prosecutor would, at least allow me to witness the jury return the verdict. Kim spoke to my advocate. She had already talked to the prosecutor regarding this matter and he gave permission to attend. Without hesitation, Kim and I rushed out of the house and headed straight for the courthouse.

When we got there, everyone including the media, seemed to be milling around, waiting for the jury. The prosecutor came over to me and took my hand. "No matter what the outcome, just keep yourself under control." He said. He seemed a little too confident to doubt he had lost this case. There was too much evidence against the defendant, including an eyewitness.

It took the jury three hours to come to a decision. The word spread rapidly throughout that the verdict was in. Court officers, cameramen, news reporters, and everyone else began to run to the courtroom door. I followed behind them. When I got to the entrance, I was stopped dead in my tracks by a barrage of deputies. They began patting me down and running a metal detector all over my body. One of the newspaper photographers took a picture of this embarrassing scene.

I quietly took a seat. I was about four feet away from the defendant. He was handcuffed and shackled again, with his head facing the floor. I could not help but look at him from time to time, and think about what he had done to my daughter.

Within minutes, the judge took the bench and the jury filed in. The judge asked the jury if it had reached a decision. An older woman wearing glasses stood up and said, "Yes, we have your Honor." The bailiff went over to the lady to retrieve the piece of paper she was holding and gave it to the judge.

As he opened the folded sheet, silence fell over the courtroom. I could hear only the clicking cameras in the background.

The judge began to speak as he eyed the written verdict. On the count of aggravated murder, the defendant was found "guilty". On the count of gross abuse of a corpse, the defendant was found "guilty". On the count of tampering with evidence, the defendant was again found "guilty".

Cameras began to click and flash. I glanced over at the defendant who just sat there, showing no emotion. His mother and family, who sat there with their heads hanging down, rushed out of the room. The judge asked everyone to calm down because he had decided to pass down the sentence now.

The judge asked the defendant if there was anything he wished to say before he passed sentence upon him. The now convicted killer didn't say a word. The judge looked at me and asked if there was anything I would like to say. I stood up and stated my name loud and proud and announced that I was Virginia's father. I told the judge not even this conviction could bring my daughter back, but that what he could do for me and the community was to impose the harshest sentence allowable by law so that this demon-monster would never hurt or kill another child again.

The judge gave the defendant twenty years to life for the charge of aggravated murder, three years for gross abuse of a corpse, and one year for the tampering with evidence. The sentences were to run consecutively which would ensure that he would *never* get out of prison.

Throughout the entire trial, and as the deputies led him away to begin a life in prison he showed no remorse. I hoped never to lay eyes on him again.

The judge hit his gavel and everything was over. Finally, all of the hearings, the fact of having to look at that murderer, all the delays, the trial and everything that brought me such aggravation had come to an end.

When I stepped out of the courtroom, the media surrounded me, trying to get my reaction. I answered them as quickly and politely as I could. I was anxious to get out of there. I pushed my way through the crowd to look for Kim. Because seating was limited, she had to watch the whole thing on a closed circuit TV in another room. I wanted to hug her and go home. I hugged my advocate and rushed out the door, hoping to never step foot into that building again.

As we made our way to the car, the reporters continued to follow us. I stopped for one of them and agreed to give a live interview for the 5 o'clock news. I wanted to announce to the world that justice for Virginia had been served.

The next day, there was a picture of the defendant of the front page of the newspaper. Below the picture, in huge print, it read, "A monster is off the streets." A reporter had stolen my words. Next to the article was a picture of me being searched by a deputy.

A big question still loomed in my mind. Was justice really served in that courtroom? Although I knew that this monster would spend the rest of his life in prison, I also knew that I would spend the rest of my life without my child.

Later, through court transcript and news reporters, I learned one juror fainted as the prosecutor displayed a poster-sized picture of my daughter's body. The juror suffered no injuries and regained her composure, but was dismissed from her duties. As the prosecutor continued pointing to the wounds on my daughter's neck, another juror vomited. The court was recessed until the maintenance crew cleaned the jury box. The young lady was allowed to continue as a juror.

On the second day a DNA expert testified that blood found on a pair of shoelaces and a pillowcase did in fact match the blood taken from my daughter during the autopsy.

Later that morning a detective testified that the shoelaces matched the other laces found in the basement of the defendant's home. He also testified that the pillowcase matched the sheet on his bed. The prosecutor asked him how he had found the evidence. The detective explained how he was led to a dumpster nearby the defendant's home by the juvenile who had been involved in the crime. The detective continued to explain that in the pillowcase were the shoelaces believed to be the murder weapon, my daughter's clothing and her gym shoes, along with a sterling silver necklace.

In the afternoon the prosecutor called Virginia's mother to the stand. She testified that the clothing, a black shirt and a pair of white jeans, as well the gym shoes belonged to our daughter. When the prosecutor showed her the sterling silver necklace, she began to cry uncontrollably. I was told one of the jurors, an older gray haired gentleman used a handkerchief to wipe his tears. After Virginia's mother regained her composure, she told the prosecutor the necklace was a gift she had given our daughter on her 14th birthday.

On the third day the eyewitness was called to the stand. He testified as to the presence of Virginia at the defendant's home at about 6:00 P.M., on Tuesday, November 23rd, 1999. Virginia and the defendant had gone to the basement, which the defendant had turned, into his sleeping quarters. He was watching television upstairs and was unaware of why they had gone to the basement.

Moments later he heard them arguing and he went to the top of the basement stairs to see why all the commotion. He witnessed the defendant on top of my daughter as he strangled her to death using the pair of shoelaces, as he pointed to the prosecutor's table.

The prosecutor asked him to recreate what he had seen. The juvenile stepped down from the witness stand and began to show what he had seen. As he recounted the crime scene, some of the jurors turned their faces away, not wanting to see anymore of the graphic details being shown. The defendant remained with his head bowed down through the entire trial.

The eyewitness was asked why he didn't help Virginia. He explained that he froze "dead in his tracks." He became fearful for his own life and the defendant would kill him next. He continued testifying that afterwards the defendant had asked him for help in disposing of her body. Together they disrobed her, dragged her outside to the wooded area and set her body on fire. They placed her clothes, her gym shoes, her necklace and the shoelaces in the pillowcase and placed it in the dumpster.

A neighbor called the fire department, and they put the fire out, they found the body of my child.

At the end of the eyewitness's testimony, the prosecutor rested his case. The defense attorney rarely objected throughout the trial. Not calling any witnesses, the defense also rested its case.

The following morning, closing arguments were made. The prosecutor recounted all the testimonies and evidence. The defense attorney asked the jury to use their best judgement in deliberating the case.

The jury was then taken to a room to begin their task. It was then I was allowed to enter the courtroom for the reading of the verdict and the sentencing.

I am glad that I was barred from the courtroom. If I had been there to see those poster-sized pictures of my daughter's body, and hear the graphic details of her death, no one would have been able to stop me from imposing my own brand of justice.

11
Memories and Momentos

Now that the trial was over and all the hype surrounding it had died down, I began to look toward the future. I knew that I would be in for some very sad times, but I also knew that I had hope to find peace and maybe even some joy.

I hadn't realized the changes that had taken place in just a little over a year. Both my sons had turned of age and had moved out into the world to live on their own. No longer, were they just around the corner. I looked out of the front room window, not only to look for Virginia, but also to see the emptiness the neighborhood now held. I no longer felt the need to live there.

After discussing my feelings with Kim, we decided to move. We bought a house in the country with plenty of room, plenty of space, and most importantly, plenty of privacy.

My favorite room is the glass-enclosed patio that sits at the rear of the house. I get up early to have my coffee and watch the sun rise over the trees in the distance.

I try not to take anything for granted these days, not a sunrise or a sunset, and especially not my wife and children. I treasure each moment I spend with them. In the family room, there are many pictures of Virginia, I like the idea that all I have to do is look around the room and see her. On the bookshelf, is an ashtray that she made for me in the 4th grade. It doesn't look much like an ashtray, but to me it's a priceless work of art. Now and then, I'll pick up and look at the bottom where she had etched her name. I hold it close to me because I know her hands shaped this masterpiece. Upstairs in my bedroom closet, I have a wooden box I call my treasure chest. It contains many things Virginia gave me over the years. There's a blue hair tie that she used to pull back her beautiful hair into a ponytail. There are pictures that she drew for me during her elementary school days. I keep the key to her casket there along with other keepsakes I've collected over the years. One item, in particular is my favorite. It's a picture of a little girl holding the hand of a man. I recall the day she bought that picture and handed it to me as she sat on my lap. I picked it up and before I had a chance to unfold it she blurted out, "It's us daddy!" Across the top of the picture she had written, "Just me and my dad."

In a small can that once contained candy, I keep the first tooth she ever lost. I remember that day every time I look at it. The children and I had gathered together to watch TV. We sat on the floor eating pizza. Before she took a bite of her slice, she yanked the tooth right out of her mouth and handed it to me. She got up off the floor and started crying. "I want my tooth back, Daddy, please, put it back!" she cried. She ran into the bathroom and I followed her. I lifted her up onto the vanity, gently wiped her tears, and began to explain why her baby tooth had fallen out. I told her she had to lose her baby teeth to get her grown up teeth. I looked into her big brown eyes and said, "You're going to be a grown up real soon!" She smiled so broadly that I couldn't help but laugh at the gap where her tooth once had been.

Also, in the closet, hangs a pair of Virginia's favorite jeans she left behind one day. There's a T-shirt she used to lounge around in to watch TV. It's worn and tattered but on occasion I'11 proudly wear it. Somehow, it makes me feel closer to her.

But what means the most to me is a burgundy, hooded sweater. She had this on the last time I saw her. It still smells like her. I've shed a million tears on that sweater and before my life is over, I'll probably shed a million more. Sometimes, I'll place the sleeves around my neck and rock back and forth with it much in the way I used to rock with Virginia. At times, I am content to stand there and hold it, taking deep breathes into it, trying to capture her scent. Often times, I fall to my knees and shed even more tears on it. Even though it is stained with my sorrow, I refuse to have it laundered. I'm afraid I'll never smell her sweet fragrance again.

When I die, I want all these mementos with me. Virginia gave them to me. They were meant for me and no one else.

I think about her dreams and how I wished to see her fulfill them someday. Shortly after Virginia entered high school, she made a decision that she would be a teacher. She hurried to my house that day to tell me the news. Of course, I was happy for her, until she told me that she planned to get her degree at a Florida university. I couldn't imagine her being so far away, but if it's what she truly wanted to do, I was prepared to support her.

Once, I was on my way to work and Virginia was at my house. Her mother's house was along my path so I offered to give her a ride. I pulled up and watched as she crossed the street. Out of nowhere, four or five of the neighborhood kids suddenly surrounded her. She made sure she hugged each and every one of them. As she stood there rubbing their heads, a little guy came running towards her with his hands up in the air just as fast as his little legs could carry him. He kept yelling "Gina! … Gina!" He was too little to call her Virginia. She lifted him up in the air and hugged him closely.

Watching this scene unfold before me, I knew she had made the right choice for her career in teaching. She had the patience, and definitely the love. She once said that she had enough love in her heart to fix anything and everything in the world. After seeing her with those children, I believed her.

I believe Virginia would have made a difference in the lives of the kids she would have taught She taught me many things. She taught me about the love of an innocent child towards her father. She taught me how to accept love without question.

I have yet to visit the cemetery where Roy's ashes sit. I'd rather keep my old friend alive in my memories and in my heart. I miss him terribly.

I have yet to visit the mausoleum where my daughter is entombed. To see her picture there with her name written in bright gold lettering across that marble stone is too stark a reminder of the reality that she is gone, a reality that I just can't bring myself to accept.

They say that time has a way of healing all wounds. Maybe it does in some cases, but the wound I carry will never heal. I don't want that kind of time left on this earth.

Every now and then, I'll still catch myself looking out the front room window, hoping to see. my daughter walking up the driveway. Even though we moved I still have hopes that she will find me. It's a hope I'll never give up. I know I'll see my little girl again. Maybe not on this earth, but I know in my heart, I will see her again.

I have long since given up on my thoughts of suicide. To commit suicide would have sent a message to my wife and children that their lives were meaningless to me. That is far from the truth. They mean everything to me. It was because of their love and support and that of God, I was able to stay strong when I had every reason to give up. Whenever I spend time with them, I try to reassure them of that truth.

There are times when my children come to visit me. Sometimes I'll have on Virginia's shirt. As they embrace me, I feel they're not only embracing me but also the T-shirt their sister once wore.

While we're sitting in the family room watching television, I see them looking at Virginia's picture. I see the mistiness in their eyes. I feel their hearts, like mine, breaking at the loss of their little sister.

They rarely mention her or recall any memories they have. I think they fear I'll hurt even more than I already have. I neither encourage nor discourage them from talking about their sister. They know I'll be there if they should ever need to hold a compassionate hand or need a loving embrace.

Seven months after my daughter died, her friends and the student council were given permission to plant an evergreen tree in front of the high school. Hundreds of kids gathered on a rainy April afternoon for the tree planting ceremony.

The principal of the high school announced he was dedicating this particular area to the memory of those who have passed away during their days at the high school. Teachers and students would be honored here with a pine tree.

"Let us pray this will be the only tree planted here. From this day forth this area will be known at Angels Acres."

I threw in the first shovel of ground that began planting the tree. My ex-wife, and the rest of the student body followed me. All of the kids were crying as they honored and remembered their friend.

During the Christmas holidays, and on her birthday and at Easter, I decorate that tree with roses. I know my Virginia would have loved that gesture. I know she does, she's with me always.

12
Reasons For Writing This Book

Every morning I would drag myself out of bed. I would wave or throw a kiss toward my daughter's picture as I crossed the living room into the kitchen to make some coffee.

One morning, as I walked past her picture, I stopped abruptly. I felt a strange sense that she wanted me to come closer. I walked slowly toward her picture, not knowing what was about to happen.

I looked at her picture intently. Suddenly, it was as though her mind was telling my mind to write a book. I sat on the sofa pondering this strange phenomenon that I had experienced. Was this really happening or was it just my imagination?

I wondered why she had chosen me and not her mother. Why not her grandparents?

Furthermore, I had no experience in writing a book. The only writing I had done was term papers in college and about a one hundred page thesis in graduate school.

I dismissed the idea as just my imagination running wild.

I feared that if I wrote a book disclosing the most tragic event in my life, people would think I was exploiting my daughter's death and revealing our most intimate secrets.

Weeks went by, but I couldn't bring myself to begin writing. I didn't know how to begin or what I would write.

On another morning, in that stage of waking up but still asleep, I heard myself saying "You'd better get busy on that book." I could no longer ignore the request my daughter had made. I began to recall events in our relationship that brought us so close.

I remembered the time she stood with her arms folded in front of her impatiently waiting for me to assemble her big wheel. I remember the smile on her face as I taught her to pedal and she began flying up and down the sidewalk waving as she passed me by.

I thought about that fall day when the leaves had fallen into a huge pile in the backyard. Both of us ran into that pile and hid from each other. I found her, picked her up, and began brushing the autumn leaves from her hair. "How did you find me daddy?" she asked. I remember telling her daddies can always find their little girls.

I used to take her to the park and push her on the swing until my arms got too tired to push anymore. She'd quickly run over to the merry-go-round and beg me to make her go 'round. I'd push that merry-go-round until she asked me to stop because she thought she was going to throw up.

I remember taking her to lunch where she would confide in me about a crush she had on a little boy in their classroom. I never laughed or made fun of her. Instead I'd tell her it was normal for little girls to have crushes on boys and for boys to have crushes on girls.

When Virginia was about twelve years old, her relationship with her mother became strained. Her mother became threatened at the fact that Virginia was becoming too close to Kim. They would spend hours on the phone talking about their favorite soap operas. They would make popcorn and watch television until her curfew, and then Kim would take her home. They were becoming very close much to the dismay of her mother. I couldn't understand her mother's's disapproval. Where would a child be safer than in her father's house?

Many times she would knock on my door. I would open it to find her upset over an argument with her mother. I would place my arms around her and try to comfort her.

In my arms and in my house she knew that she could always find a place of refuge. She knew I would always drop what I was doing and listen to her.

Maybe that's why Virginia chose me, because she knew I would listen. Although it has been painful recalling the events that ensued after that early morning phone call, somewhere along the way I began to smile and even laugh as I recalled the fun Virginia and I shared.

Maybe that was another reason, she wanted to tell me that it was okay for me to smile and laugh again the way we did on our last day together. I want Virginia to live forever, not only in the pages of my mind and within the beats of my heart, but in the pages of a book she inspired.

<u>Father's Day Letter from Virginia June 15, 1977</u>

TO: Father
LOCATION: Amber's
Date: June 15, 1997   FROM: Virginia Velez

SUBJECT: Gratitude

Dear Dad,

First of all I want to say how sorry I am for forgetting about your day. But as upset as I am, I'm filled with joy. Because I know how lucky I am 2-have a father like you! I look around me, at my friends, some of their fathers are in jail, some of their fathers just don't care but when I look back at my father he's always there!

I feel bad because I know I take you 4-granted. But don't think I don't care. I may mess up a lot, <**> hate

your lectures when I get them, but just remember I'd rather you be lecturing me than not be there at all!!!!!
I Love You so much, and I'm so glad you're always there 4-me! I know this may not mean much 2-you, but I just wanted 2-make sure you know I love you!

And that I am grateful 4-everything you've done 4-me, everything!

I Love You & I pray I'll be your little munchkin 4-ever!

Love Always,

<**>

Father's day
1997

13
The Conclusion

There is no end to this story. I think of my daughter the first thing in the morning and she's the last thing on my mind before I go to bed. During the time between, I cling to the beautiful memories she left behind, but mostly, I cling to the Lord for dear life. It is through Him that I have found my truest comfort. It is through Him that I have found some peace.

I still struggle with depression, but I don't let it control me. I control it. I'm not only a fighter, I'm a winner. It has been well over a year since I saw that man in the mirror. I'm still holding true to the promise I made to him that day, and to my daughter.

I couldn't stop wondering how my daughter became acquainted with this monster. I conducted my own investigation into the history of this would be killer.

I found that he began his criminal career at the age of nine. He started by breaking storefront windows, committing petty theft and damaging parked cars. At 12 years of age he graduated to carrying concealed weapons, possession of drugs and had been charged with disorderly conduct. By the time he was fifteen his mother had him arrested for beating her. He was charged with domestic violence, but was released back to the custody of his mother. Shortly thereafter he brutally beat his girlfriend who spent two weeks in the hospital recovering from a broken jaw and an internal injury.

He was arrested for aggravated assault, but again the juvenile authorities released him to his mother.

I was told by his neighbors and some people that knew him, that his mother had finally thrown her hands up in disgust at her son's behavior and no longer made any attempts to correct or discipline him. I heard no mention of his father's whereabouts. No one seemed to know who he was or where he had gone.

It appeared that the juvenile authorities had failed to intervene on his behalf and continued to allow him to get away with murder. They offered him no counseling. His crime spree went unpunished, with the exception of being placed in a detention home for a short period of time.

In school he was failing miserably. Although he managed to make passing grades with some subjects, a soon to be eighteen year old man was taking a freshman English class. Unfortunately, he sat next to my fifteen-year old daughter.

He befriended my daughter by asking her to help him with his homework, a task Virginia was eager to help with for anyone who would ask. However, soon they were seen not only in the library studying, but also in the cafeteria having lunch together. On some occasions he was seen walking her home.

Virginia's friends warned her of his criminal record and his violent nature. Upon hearing how he had beaten his former girlfriend, my daughter began to shun the attentions of that monster. The rejection only served to infuriate him. He continued to call her and page her but my daughter did not return his calls and pages.

Two days after Virginia turned fifteen years old, he called on the pretense of having a gift for her. Unsuspecting of what was going to happen, she allowed him to lure her into the basement of that duplex. I believed Virginia never disclosed to me the problem she was having with that monster. She knew I would protect her in a way that would have landed me in jail. That's why I never heard her mention his name.

Some mornings, when I'm sitting on the patio getting ready to watch another sunrise, I'11 begin to cry for no other reason that the fact that I miss my child and all the things we had yet to experience. I miss her smile. I miss the laughter she had when we used to joke and clown around. I miss the way she used to take my arms and put them around her. I miss hearing her whisper in my ear, "I love you daddy," Mainly, I miss the joy she brought to my life.

I look around at all of the yard work that still needs to be done. I know that Roy would have been here helping me, making an occasional trip to the beer cooler. He always had something funny to say. I miss my old friend and all the times we had shared together. At least I know that once upon a time, I had a dear and close friend who I trusted with my life.

Sometimes, I feel terribly alone, but almost as if on cue, Kim will engage me in some conversation and put an ease to my feeling. I wonder if she can sense my loneliness.

I once read a passage in a book that said, "Your future lies in the choices and plans you make today…" There's a lot of truth in that statement, but sometimes certain events take place in your life that dictate your plans, choices, and even your future. I know this too well.

I was a happy-go-lucky working stiff, trying to help raise my children so that one day they could stand on their own two feet, independent and self-sufficient. I would retire and move south where the climate is warm year round, and I would live happily ever after.

Instead, I faced a tragedy that has changed my life forever. I have been in places I had only seen on TV. I have experienced feelings I never knew I had. I met people I had only read about or seen in the news. I heard and learned things I didn't care to know about at all.

Sometimes, I' 11 smile and even try to laugh, but anyone with a sense of perception can easily see that it's just an attempt at being polite. I doubt I'll ever regain the smiles and the laughter that once used to come from within.

One day, my time will come. It will be my turn to go home. The Lord will call my name and swoop me up into his loving arms. We will share a laugh. He will take me through the air to His Kingdom. There, we will walk down a country-like path. There will be flower gardens the likes of which no artist has yet to capture. The sun will be shining for me. As we continue our walk, I will feel his hand in mind. In the distance, I'll see a figure walking towards us. I will catch a glimpse of that beautiful, long, brown hair. The Lord will look down upon me and say, "Go and be reunited with your daughter," I will run towards her and she will run towards me. We will embrace and I will hear her whisper in my ear, "I love you, daddy." I will stroke her hair and kiss her face and touch her beautiful, heartshaped lips. I will take in a deep breath and, once again capture the fragrance of a "rose".

Reviews

This compelling and moving book shows how a father's love for his daughter helps him conquer her loss and his depression.

Robert D. Eppley, M.D.
Psychiatry

~~~~~~~~~

And emotional rollercoaster of a read. A valued experience of shared grief and the long and winding road back. A special meaning for persons who may have suffered the loss...of a child. A "therapy" for both the writer and the reader.

Dr. Mark McKinley, ED. D.

~~~~~~~~~

This book is not only about the loss of a child it is also a story about a relationship between a father and his daughter. The loss of the authors daughter sends him into an abyss of depression and explains how he managed to rise to the surface, making this book a source of therapeutic value.

Mr. Velez reaches into his inner soul in expressing his turmoil. It sends shivers through me as I read of how he is dealing with such a profound loss, while holding unto his spiritual roots. The innocence and sometimes sentimental overview lends a genuine love of a father for his daughter.

This book is a must read for anyone who has lost a child, or having relationship problems with their children. The way in which the author ends the book gives hope that everyone can cling to.

Adrian Johnston, Book Review

About the Author

Louis M. Velez was born in Lares, Puerto Rico. He came to Lorain, Ohio with his parents one year later. He was raised in the South Lorain area.

Upon graduation from Admiral King High School he enlisted in the U.S. Navy serving two tours of duty in Vietnam.

Louis returned and graduated from Lorain County Community College and Baldwin College with degrees in secondary education.

He now lives a quiet and peaceful life in Elyria where he is working on another book. He continues to compile a collection of poetry and will have it published in the near future.